IMAGES
of America

CRESTLINE

CREST FOREST—"THE PLAYGROUND OF THE SKY"

CREST FOREST comprises some forty-five square miles of forest wonderland recognized as one of the outstanding beauty spots of the Southland. As its name implies, it is located along the Crest of the famous San Bernardino Mountains in a truly forest primeval that commands the most scenic views of the Orange Empire on one side and the beautiful and awe-inspiring Mohave Desert on the other.

During the Winter Season a heavy blanket of snow mantles the great oaks and giant pines and makes it an attractive place to enjoy a frolic amid wintry scenes. Come and play with us at your favorite winter sport. Skiing, Tobogganing, Snowshoeing, Skating, snow ball fights and in fact any well known winter sport is at your command in Crest Forest. In all the world no spot like this.

CREST FOREST CLUB, CRESTLINE, CALIFORNIA

The Crest Forest Club preceded the chamber of commerce in advertising the recreational value of the Crestline area in the early 1920s.

ON THE COVER: The Pork-e-Pines cabin was typical of the style of vacation homes built in Crestline during the 1920s. A Valley of Enchantment developer stands to the right of the stairway.

IMAGES
of America

CRESTLINE

Rhea-Frances Tetley

ARCADIA
PUBLISHING

Published by Arcadia Publishing
Charleston, South Carolina

Library of Congress Catalog Card Number: 2005932378

For all general information contact Arcadia Publishing at:
Telephone 843-853-2070
Fax 843-853-0044
E-mail sales@arcadiapublishing.com
For customer service and orders:
Toll-Free 1-888-313-2665

Visit us on the Internet at www.arcadiapublishing.com

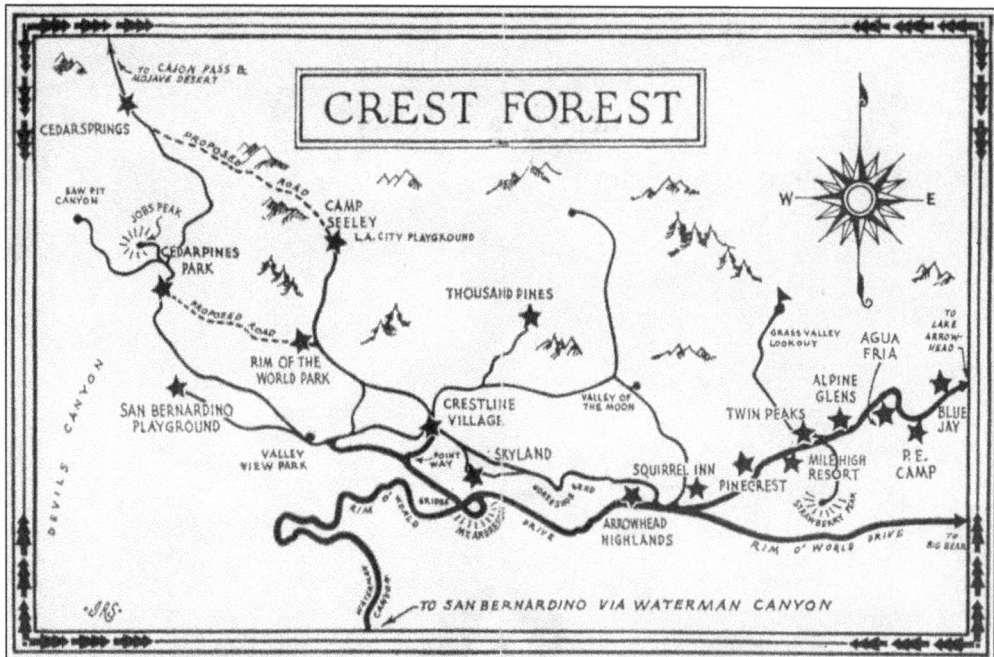

This c. 1927 map of the Crest Forest area appeared in an advertising brochure by the Crest Forest developers and resort owners.

CONTENTS

ACKNOWLEDGMENTS

So many people have helped me not only with this book project, but also in all aspects of my life that led to the creation of this book. I want to thank each of them, but it would take an entire book just to mention them all. I want each of you to know I appreciate your input and encouragement.

I want to thank my parents, Ruth and Richard Tetley, my grandparents and great-grandparents, and my great-aunt Frances Tetley Harthan for sharing with me the rich history of the San Bernardino Mountains and for choosing such a beautiful area to develop.

I want to thank my husband of 32 years, Douglas Motley, for his encouragement and editing skills. Our children, Sean and David Motley, for being their individual selves, and Katie and Amelia for adding to our family. Thank you Dennis Labadie, owner/publisher of *The Alpenhorn News*, for printing my weekly ramblings on Crestline's history and especially for the generous use of his scanners and computers.

Thanks to the Rim of the World Historical Society, especially its president, W. Lee Cozad, and Mary Barlow. Stan Bellamy, Don Foster, J. Putnam Henck, and Pauliena LaFuze—I thank each of you for sharing your memories with me and inspiring and encouraging me to write about the San Bernardino Mountains. Most of all, thank you Tom Powell Jr. for inviting me to help start the Crest Forest Historical Society in the 1980s. If not for you, I would never have collected these photographs and stories. There are so many who have assisted me, and I apologize for not mentioning each of you by name, but I am grateful for your support.

This book is dedicated to my late father, Richard Alan Tetley Sr., who as a young boy learned to drive a tractor while cutting in roads on his family's Valley of Enchantment subdivision. I'm especially grateful to him for sharing his memories of the construction of Lake Gregory. He always encouraged me and told me I was capable of whatever I set my mind to do. He told me the stories of the "good old days" of Crestline, and without his insightful knowledge of the development of the Crestline community, my interest and understanding of the area's history would not be as complete. Thank you, Daddy!

—Rhea-Frances Tetley

PHOTOGRAPH CREDITS

A—*The Alpenhorn News* photograph files of Dennis Labadie, publisher
CC—Lake Arrowhead Chamber of Commerce
DR—collection of Diane Rosen
G—donated by Cathy Gamble
GC—donated by Gene and Jane Cuthberson
LR—taken by Lee Reeder
R—Rim of the World Historical Society
S—donated by Lural Schafer
T—collection of Rhea-Frances Tetley and family

Other photographs are individually credited in the book.

INTRODUCTION

Crestline is located at the 4,700-foot level of the San Bernardino Mountains, surrounded by the San Bernardino National Forest. The town's history parallels that of the rest of California, as lumber from Crestline was used to build Southern California's cities and towns. The area has also supported the vacation and residential needs of the valley below. Living in the area affords the unusual experience of a small mountain town separated by climate, elevation, history, and distance from the typical congested, hectic Southern California lifestyle just minutes away by highway. How and why is Crestline unique? Is it the altitude or its attitude?

Crestline was a summer home to the Serrano Indians, who came to the mountains to escape the heat of the desert floor. The Serranos lived in family groups and, being hunter-gathers, moved with the ripening of their favorite nuts and berries. One village was located in the meadow of the Valley of Enchantment, near Seeley Creek, which was one of the first places the Mormons would later settle. The Spanish first entered the area when Juan Bandini went to Sawpit Canyon to cut lumber near Cedar Pines Park, but he didn't stay or disrupt the lifestyle of the Serrano Indians. Life for the tribe changed after Mormon settlers built permanent sawmills in the Crestline area in the mid-1850s. After the Battle of Indian Hill near Blue Jay in 1867, the Serranos moved out of the area.

When Mormon settlers came to California, Don Antonio Lugo sold them his cattle ranch, which he called Rancho San Bernardino. The colony's Mormon leaders decided they also needed a stockade to protect themselves from area Native Americans who were known to steal horses and livestock, and they eyed the tall pines along the crest of the mountains. In 1852, the colony built a road up the steep southern front of the mountain to harvest the lumber, which was sold to construct buildings in towns throughout California. Hollowed-out logs were the first pipes for the water system of Los Angeles.

The harvested lumber became known as "Mormon Currency," as many church members paid for their land by the sale of lumber from the mountains. Then, in 1857, the Mormon faithful were recalled to Salt Lake City by Brigham Young, and 60 percent of the colony's families sold their sawmills for pennies on the dollar. As the mills were sold, new lumbermen came to the mountains to reap the plentiful lumber harvest. Two new lumber roads were built to the mountains by 1870.

When the Arrowhead Reservoir Company decided to build a lake in Little Bear Valley (now Lake Arrowhead), the area now known as Old Town Crestline became the stopping point at the end of a long climb to the crest. A corral was built next to a cement storage warehouse to allow the oxen and horses to rest, and the area became known as "Flycamp." An incline cable rail system was also built to the summit of the Skyland area of Crestline to hasten the delivery of the heavy bags of cement destined to build the dam in Little Bear Valley.

The establishment of the San Bernardino National Forest by Pres. Grover Cleveland in 1891 led to the closing of some of the lumber mills. Homesteads began to appear where former timber tracts had been. The forest was used for camping by valley residents wanting to escape the sizzling heat of summer. As the movie industry began, silent movie producers found the mountains an excellent four-season, varied-terrain location not far from Hollywood that had campgrounds and hotels for the crews and stars. The only movie studio that was built in the San Bernardino Mountains was in Crestline in an area called Skyland Flats, by cowboy star Leo Maloney.

Crestline received its name in 1919, when postmaster Samuel Dillin moved the Skyland Post Office to the cement warehouse, where Highway 138 and Crest Forest Drive now cross in Old Town Crestline. The "Subdivision Era" began as Charles S. Mann built roads and developed lots for vacation use, and the town came to life as merchants supplied the needs of visitors and residents alike. The Rim O' the World Club, a fire department, and schools were established in 1929, and the High Gear Road (Highway 18) was built, with an access road (Highway 138) leading directly to Crestline in 1933.

During the Depression, Camp Seeley, owned and operated by the City of Los Angeles, was occupied during the summer months by homeless families. Lake Gregory was built in the late 1930s to provide a steady supply of water to the area. World War II found the vacation homes in Crestline used as residential housing for Norton Air Force Base personnel. Murphy's Dance Hall and others were used for rest and relaxation by military personnel.

After the war, a population boom occurred, as the exclusive Club San Moritz began marketing and selling thousands of vacation home lots around Lake Gregory to upscale visitors. Club San Moritz was a successful influence in the town for over 30 years, promoting an alpine theme. Crestline was aptly called "The Alps of Southern California," and the town hosted a post office called Switzerland next to the Club San Moritz Lodge building in the Valley of the Moon.

The 1960s saw the construction of a four-lane highway to the Crestline interchange, opening up direct access to the mountaintop and making it a new commuter-friendly residential community. The population has grown steadily since the completion of Highway 18 to Crestline, with approximately 14,000 full-time residents now calling the mountain paradise home. On holiday weekends, the number of people in town can swell to over 100,000 as the motels and vacation homes fill with visitors. So is it the altitude or the attitude that makes Crestline unique? It is a reflection of its history and the people who make Crestline their home, so probably it's a combination of the two.

One

ON THE CREST
OF THE MOUNTAIN

The arrowhead geological formation on the hillside at the entrance of Waterman Canyon, which is passed when coming to Crestline, is 1,275 feet long, 449 feet wide, and covers seven-and-a-half acres. The sandy, quartz soil in its interior will only grow light-colored sage, not the natural dark green vegetation covering the rest of the mountainside, so its color contrast makes the hillside look like an arrowhead. It points to a hot spring in the canyon below it. (T.)

The Indian statue on Old Waterman Canyon Road honors the Native Americans who lived in the area and was created in the 1920s by Joseph Leeland Roop for the Arrowhead Springs Hotel's entrance archway. The mineral hot springs were believed by the Indians to contain healing powers and were considered sacred. After a battle, both sides would take their wounded to this neutral ground. (T.)

The statue's arm pointed in the direction of the arrowhead landmark, hot springs, and steam caves, and the sites of four hotels built at the hot springs over the years. Restored by the Native Sons (#110) and Daughters (#241) of the Golden West, the statue was placed in its current location in 1976 after the entrance arch was removed for the construction of the four-lane-wide Highway 18 in the 1960s. (T.)

Indian arrowheads have been found in many places in the Crestline area, especially in the meadows near creeks. Stone mortars above have been found in Sawpit Canyon. There were also Indian encampments in the Camp Seeley area of the Valley of Enchantment and the Huston Flat area, near present-day Lake Gregory. (T.)

The Indians spent the spring, summer, and early fall gathering acorns and pinion nuts and hunting small game in the mountains. The peaceful hunter-gatherer Serrano Indians wintered in the desert north of the mountains. They lived in brush huts in family villages of 25 to 60 people. They cooked we-wish, an acorn mush, by heating rocks in a fire and transferring the hot rocks to baskets filled with water and ground acorn meal. (T.)

11

The first man to travel to California overland from the East was Father Garces, who traveled from Arizona to Mission San Gabriel over the San Bernardino Mountains. He crossed through Sawpit and Devil's Canyon using the Mojave Indian Trail, observing the Pacific Ocean from Monument Peak near current-day Cedar Pines Park in March 1776. Monument Peak was named in 1931, when the San Bernardino County Historical Society placed this marker. (T.)

Just 50 years later, Jedediah Strong Smith, an American Mountain Man, traveled overland from Salt Lake City and was led along the Mojave Indian Trail trading route through the mountains, sighting the Pacific Ocean from Monument Peak in November 1826. He was exhausted from the journey and was nursed back to health at the Assistencia, near Redlands. This drawing of Jed Smith at Monument Peak in 1826 is from the *Rim of the World Historical* Coloring Book. (T.)

12

The first non-Indian to use the resources of the mountains was Juan Bandini, who began cutting lumber near current-day Sawpit Canyon in 1839 to gain access up the Indian Trail. He used the wood to build frames to support the roofs of the adobe buildings. Sawpit Canyon got its name from this mill, where one man would stand down in a hole (the sawpit) and another on top of the log. Walking along the length of the log, they used a long saw to cut the wood into slabs. (T.)

The Mormon colony wanted the timber they noticed along the crest of the mountains they called the "Sierra Nevadas" and decided to build a road to reach it, up through Hot Springs Canyon. They spent a total of 1,000 man-days in about 10 days in 1852 building the 12-mile road to the summit with picks and shovels. Capt. David Seely then built a sawmill in what is now the Valley of Enchantment and sent logs used to build the Mormon colony down to San Bernardino. In 1922, this monument was placed by the Native Sons of the Golden West in the park on Crest Forest Drive across from the Crestline Tavern and Post Office, to mark the success of that feat. (T.)

13

David Seely and his brother Wellington, from the Mormon colony in San Bernardino, built the first mountaintop sawmill, powered by Seeley Creek (the spelling of Seely was somehow changed to Seeley at the turn of the 20th century) in the area now known as the Valley of Enchantment, in 1852. The lumber was also sold to pay the $77,500 that the colony owed to purchase the Rancho San Bernardino. Camp Seeley sits on the old sawmill site, and this monument can be found in the parking lot. (T.)

Within a couple of years, there were four more sawmills in the Seely Flat area. Charles Crismon brought a steam engine up the Mormon Road in 1853 and set up a sawmill where Lake Gregory Village sits. Bishop William Crosby and Mormon Taylor operated a water-powered mill near the east end of the valley where Lake Gregory is now located. All the mills worked for the benefit of their owners and the colony. David Seely, pictured here, became a county supervisor and served from 1869 to 1873. (T.)

14

In 1857, the Mormon faithful were called back to Salt Lake City and thus sold their mills quickly and cheaply. The sawmills continued to operate and expand as technology advanced. The Crestline area was never clear-cut, as were other areas in the mountains. This Dolbeer steam engine was used to move huge logs to the mill. A cable would be strung around standing trees, and the winch would drag the sledded engine and logs over rough terrain. (T.)

The lumber sent down the mountain became known as "Mormon Currency," as enough lumber was sold to build over 700 buildings in Los Angeles between 1854 and 1856. The pipes for Los Angeles's first water system were bored-out logs from Mormon mills. Unfortunately, they kept springing leaks at the joints. This Mormon lumber wagon was restored by Greg Dexter in the 1950s and is located on Highway 189 in Twin Peaks. (T.)

Job's Peak got its name during the logging era when, after performing heavy hauling, the oxen were allowed to graze, and an ox named Job would often wander up to a peak not far away from the Seely Flat Sawmill. When he was needed, Seely would send a worker to "get Job off his peak." The peak (elevation 5,388 feet), located in what is now Cedarpines Park, became known as Job's Peak. (T.)

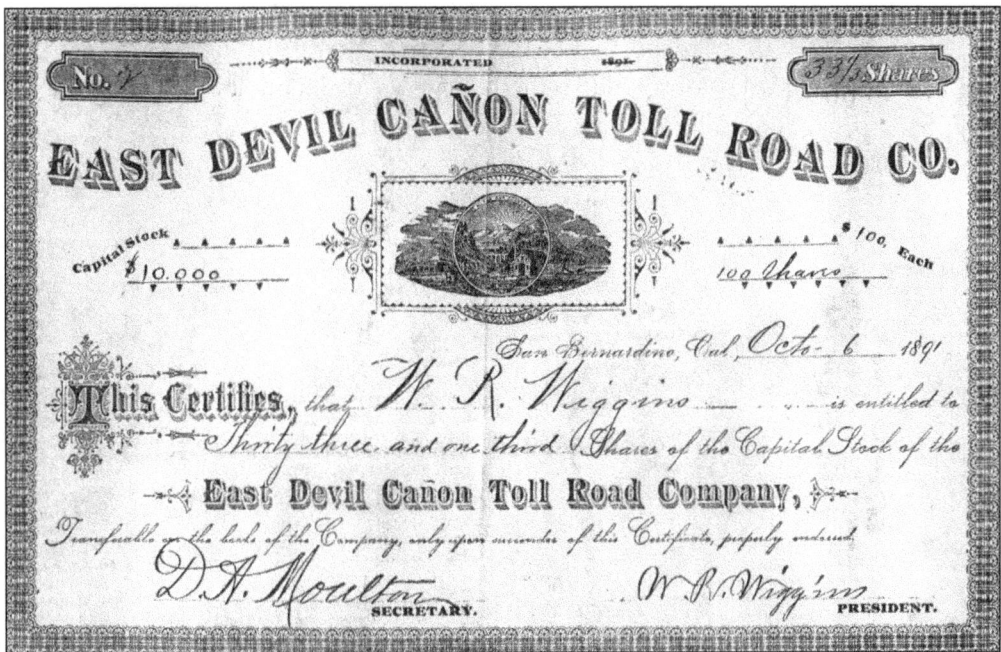

The Devil's Canyon Toll Road opened in 1879 and was used by most of the Crestline sawmills. It was constructed up through Devil's Canyon from San Bernardino to the crest, coming down into Sawpit Canyon, with the road splitting and going up to Job's Peak, over to Seely Flat (Valley of Enchantment), and continuing to Huston Flats (now under Lake Gregory). The name for Canon de El Diablo came from a story Daniel Sexton told about his trip through the canyon up to the forest to cut fencing materials. His two Indian companions were attacked and killed by "devil rattlesnakes." One of the Native Americans yelled out "el diablo" just before he died. The name has been anglicized to Devil's Canyon. (R.)

Hot Springs Canyon, through which the Mormon Road had been built, was renamed Waterman Canyon in 1892 to honor the death of Robert W. Waterman, the governor of California from 1887 to 1891 and the discoverer of silver in the Calico Hills. When Waterman bought the land, hot springs, and canyon in 1873, the Mormon Road had been abandoned for less-steep and dangerous routes to the crest, such as the 1870 Daley Canyon Road and Devil's Canyon Road, which opened in 1879. (T.)

After Governor Waterman's death in 1891, the Arrowhead Hot Springs Hotel Company bought his ranch. The Arrowhead Reservoir Company planned an extensive water project in the Little Bear Valley area to supply irrigation water to the San Bernardino Valley, diverting its natural flow. They needed to transport cement up the mountain for construction of the dam's core. The Arrowhead Company bought the road rights to the Old Mormon Road and began constructing the Arrowhead Reservoir Toll Road in 1893. This view is looking from the road, back down the canyon towards San Bernardino at the turn of the 20th century (T.)

During the 1890s, the Arrowhead Reservoir Company built a toll road through Waterman Canyon, which provided a southern access into the mountains. They transported their cement up the mountain, by horse and oxen-drawn wagons, to Little Bear Valley for the construction of a dam (that became Lake Arrowhead Dam). They built a cement holding warehouse at the crest and corrals for the horses and oxen. The warehouse, bunkhouse, and corrals became known as Fly Camp, named for the hordes of flies that congregated in the area now known as Old Town Crestline. (R.)

Oxen hauled up tons of equipment over the Arrowhead Reservoir Toll Road to the future dam site, including two narrow-gage train engines, 45 train dump cars, and steam shovels. The steepest upper (north) slope of the canyon had 13 switchbacks carved into the mountainside. It would take the drivers about 12 to 16 hours to reach the summit, as the animals needed to rest every hour. Eight horse teams hauled tons of bags of cement up the road. After resting at Fly Camp, new teams hauled the loads over to the dam site in Little Bear Valley along the approximate route of Crest Forest Drive and Highway 189. The outlet tower in Lake Arrowhead was built to control the amount of water leaving the lake that traveled through a tunnel to Willow Creek. (R.)

The 1890s saw a back-to-nature movement sweep the country as citizens rediscovered nature and the value of the watersheds. Camping became popular and a need to preserve the forests created the beginnings of the San Bernardino Forest Preserve. Skyland became a popular location for camping, as it looked out over the valley below. Vacationers used the lumber and reservoir toll roads to reach the cool, mountain air. The Skyland Inn opened in 1903. (T.)

In 1893, the Arrowhead Mountain Club, a group of prominent San Bernardino businessmen, built the Squirrel Inn, a private retreat near Sphinx Rock along the Rim. These conservative conservationists advocated for the establishment of a National Forest Preserve and hosted both John Muir and Teddy Roosevelt at their resort. (T.)

Dr. John Baylis, shown in his later years, was a member of the Squirrel Inn and acted as its treasurer. He purchased the adjoining Smithson Ranch property when it was to be logged. He built the beautiful Pinecrest Resort, opening it in 1909. Baylis became the number-one promoter of the area in the early years of the 20th century and suggested the name "Rim of the World Road." (T.)

Vacationers who wanted to escape the heat of the valleys and camp in the mountains came up the toll roads and fished the streams, hunted small game, and enjoyed the outdoors. The San Bernardino Pioneer Society, the first historical group in San Bernardino, made yearly trips to the future Crestline area. The membership requirement to become a member of the society was to move to San Bernardino prior to 1860 or be a direct descendant of someone who did. Pioneer Camp Road and Mormon Springs Road led to two of their favorite camping locations. (T.)

In 1906, San Bernardino County purchased all the private logging and toll roads and opened them free to the public, including the Arrowhead Reservoir Road that led to Crestline. This opened the mountains to many more visitors who came to visit the newly opened resorts, lodges, and campgrounds, such as Thousand Pines Camp. Stage lines already were on regular weekly routes into the mountains during most of the year to bring visitors up the mountain. (T.)

The 4,170-foot-long Incline Railway was to be powered by a donkey steam engine, placed on a cement platform at the top. The tracks, trestles, and rails were prefabricated, placed on the front of a work car, and pulled up the track by the steam engine, installing about 100 feet a day over the pre-graded route. This method proved to be very efficient, and almost two-thirds of the rails were installed before the rainstorm in June. (T.)

The storm washed out 150 feet of the graded rail bed, but installers continued to work straight through the washed-out area, creating a dip in the rails. When the first trip was made on July 31, 1906, carrying three tons of cement bags, the cable car hit the dip in the rails, resulting in the cars jumping dangerously into the air. Many loads were lost, and many corrections were attempted before the system was abandoned. The Incline tracks and trestles were destroyed in the 1911 fire. (T.)

In 1911, the first automobiles were allowed on mountain roads, but they were limited in the days and hours they could travel so the horses would not be spooked by the noisy, smelly machines on the steep and narrow mountain roads. Repairs to the road grade in some spots made it more auto-friendly. The Rim of the World Road had a grand opening in 1915, and Pinecrest Resort owner Dr. John Baylis, who campaigned for the road and named it, sponsored the event. (T.)

Waterman Can. San Bernardino Mts. 1913

The first route of the Rim of the World Road left San Bernardino and followed the old Arrowhead Reservoir Road through Waterman Canyon (shown) up the switchbacks to Clifton Heights, where the Crestline Cutoff and Crestline Road meet Crest Forest Drive. The route continued east along Crest Forest Drive, past Horseshoe Bend, out to Arrowhead Highlands and Sphinx Rock before turning inland and going past the Squirrel Inn. This route is now Highway 189. Where Pinecrest is located, it turned east again out to the rim to where the 101-mile monument is located and continued on east along the rim towards Running Springs and Green Valley to Big Bear and back down to San Bernardino. (R; T.)

SWITCHBACKS, ON "RIM-O-THE-WORLD" DRIVE.

The route to Crestline remained the same until the end of the 1920s. The switchbacks were too steep and needed replacement, as some cars had to back up the curves to keep gas in their engines because fuel pumps had not yet been invented. The 13 switchbacks were replaced by a new routing of a paved State High Gear Road across the southern mountain front, and not through Crestline. (T.)

This bypass of Crestline did not make the Crestline Chamber of Commerce happy, as the only point of entry was Arrowhead Highlands to the east of town. They sent a petition and asked the county to build them access to the new road. Crestline staked out a route and it was constructed between 1929 and 1930, along the west side of Skyland Mountain that connected at Incline Point, where the Incline Track crossed over the location of the new road. (DR.)

A bridge was required to connect the county-built road with the state's High Gear Road to keep the road grade at less than eight percent. It was a trestle-style, one-lane bridge with a stop sign at each end. The location where the bridge was built was renamed Mount Andreson, for the county supervisor who approved the road into Crestline. It had two upper terminuses, one at Clifton Heights where the switchback road came into town, and one in the center of Crestline next to the post office building. This route is now known as Highway 138. (T.)

DEDICATION OF PIONEER MONUMENT, MARKING THE MORMON TRAIL ON HIGH-GEAR ROAD, NEAR CRESTLINE, CAL. BY THURSDAY CLUB, CREST FOREST DISTRICT. Nov. 10-1932

As the new road was being completed, the Women's Thursday Club decided to place a monument where the High Gear Road crossed the old Mormon Road route. The monument was dedicated on November 10, 1932, and was inscribed "Mormon Lumber Road, Built by the Pioneers, Dedicated to the Pioneer Women of 1852 by the women of 1932, Thursday Club of Crest Forest." Giving the dedication speech is George W. Beattie, author of the book *The Heritage of the Valley*. (R.)

The last stretch of the High Gear Road was completed to Crestline on October 22, 1933. State road commissioner Frank A. Tetley Sr. cut the ribbon on the bypass of Waterman Canyon. The road was built along the west wall of the canyon instead of along the canyon bottom, where the creek had flooded it out several times. The four-and-a-half-mile section of two-lane roadway cost $350,000 to build. (T.)

The section of High Gear Road built east of the Crestline Bridge and below Skyland was created by blasting it into the steep, 80- to 90-percent-grade hillside and was considered an engineering marvel of its day. The speed limit for the state was 35 miles per hour, and people were amazed that they no longer needed to drive in the mountains in low gear, which is why it was called the Rim of the World High Gear Road. (T.)

Jan. 31. 1943

During the early 2000s, the roads suffered from numerous closures caused by falling boulders. In the years after the 2003 Old Fire, the Narrows had many landslides caused by rocks made brittle by the fire and from the heavy rains of 2005. During a recent two-year period, the road was only open a total of six months because, when it was constructed in 1929, it had not been built down to bedrock. Caltrans corrected the problems at each of 18 locations by enlarging drains, replacing collapsed roadbeds, adding screen-netting on the upper hillside, and building up washed-out areas of road. This 1943 photograph shows a landslide on the Narrows while it was still being highly touted as a "high gear road." (T.)

While the Crestline Bridge was being replaced in 1964 to make room for a four-lane highway, an earthquake fault was discovered that halted any thoughts of widening the next section of road, which was constructed below Skyland. Now known as the Narrows (because it was never widened), the road still has the same 1929 construction. Because of the sharp curves and steep upper and lower slopes, this section of road has seen many accidents from newer cars traveling too fast for road conditions. This looks at the old Crestline Bridge from the Narrows in the early 1960s. (DR.)

Two

CRESTLINE DEVELOPS

Valley residents desired the cooler air of the mountains during the extreme heat of summer. When the Arrowhead Reservoir Toll Road was built in the 1890s, whole families would pack up their wagons and camp for weeks at a time in an area they called Skyland, which overlooked the valley floor with a view of Catalina Island far in the distance. Supervisor John Andreson Sr. took his entire family camping in the Skyland area many times from the 1890s to 1910s. Crestline would later be very grateful to the Andreson family when, in 1929, John Jr. became a county supervisor and approved the construction of a connecting road from the Rim of the World High Gear Road up to Crestline (Highway 138). (T.)

This image is from a brochure that states, "Both in location and contour, Skyland Forest is essentially exclusive. Situated at an elevation, yet with more level sites than usual to mountain developments, surrounded on three sides by the U.S. Forest Reserve, commanding a magnificent view of the Great San Bernardino Valley with its city lights. Views to the north are of the Great Mojave Desert in its almost primitive naturalness. Skyland Forest is Unique." (T.)

Typical
Mountain
Homes
in
Crestline Village
and
Skyland

The same brochure continues, "Skyland Forest has some of the biggest trees in the Crest Forest district. Its residential sites are all of unusually large size and because of the many beautiful trees and the contour of the land, there is no sense of congestion, nor are rows of houses visible, each being screened to a certain extent from any group of adjacent buildings. Water is supplied by the Crestline Village Mutual Water Co., The Edison Co. furnishes electrical service to practically every part of Skyland Forest." (T.)

The Skyland Inn was a resort and twice-weekly stage stop built next to the campground in 1903. When the Arrowhead Toll Road became a free county road in 1906, even more visitors came to stay at the Skyland Inn and campground. Activities at Skyland during the early years included horseshoes, horseback riding, archery, hiking, stream fishing, and "Uncle Billy" Stevens, who would entertain the visitors with his stories and concertina. (T.)

John Hansen opened the first post office in the western San Bernardino Mountains at the Skyland Inn in June 1907 and named it Incline. The Incline Railroad was the new cable-car system, built to bring bags of cement up the face of the mountain for construction of the dam at Little Bear. Its upper terminus, where the tram engine that pulled the cable car up the mountain was located in Skyland, was not far from the post office. The name of the post office was changed to Skyland Heights in 1910 after the Incline went out of use. (T.)

The Incline Railroad was a cable-car system designed to haul heavy loads of cement up the steep, 45-degree southern face of the mountain. From Skyland, the cement would be taken by horse-drawn wagons over to construct the dams and tunnels the Arrowhead Reservoir Water Project was building in the Little Bear Valley area, now known as Lake Arrowhead. The Incline was also used a few times to send apples from the area's orchards down to market. This cement pier that held the steam engine for the Incline is still in Skyland. (T.)

Unfortunately, the 1920 government survey that Ramsay and Mann used when creating the Skyland Forest tract in 1923 conflicted with the original 1885 survey. A 1982 survey discovered the subdivision had encroached on forestland. The 17 infringing lot owners had to buy the property from the United States Forest Service (USFS) at the rate of $2,000 an acre. Only two owners had more than half of an acre of encroachment. (T.)

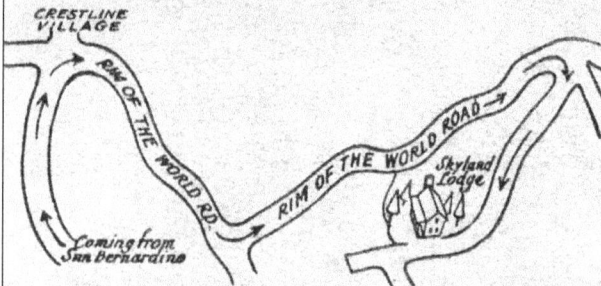

This Skyland Inn advertisement from a 1940s Crestline Stampede and Rodeo Program shows that Crest Forest Drive was then called "Rim of the World Road." Inside the program, the Club San Moritz was still advertising itself as located in Switzerland (Valley of the Moon), although the post office there had closed in 1941. (Kim Sanchez.)

The Skyland Lodge was an updated Skyland Inn. It continued to welcome visitors to its five-acre orchard and resort until it burned down in 1955. There were other bed and breakfast's in the Skyland area until the 1980s. The stairs leading to the Skyland Lodge still remains today on Skyland Drive. (T.)

Skyland was severely affected by the Old Fire of 2003, losing 35 homes because of its location on the Rim. Many other homes were scorched or suffered lost trees. The Crest Forest firefighters almost single-handedly stopped the fire on the first road from the crest, saving the entire town of Crestline. Homes are already being rebuilt in Skyland. (LR.)

In 1906, sawmill owner H. A. Guernsey attempted to build a summer vacation town in the pines. He wanted to make a profit on his sawed-over lands near the Arrowhead Reservoir Company's cement warehouse, located at the crest of Waterman Canyon where Old Town Crestline is now. The county purchased the Arrowhead Reservoir Road and opened it to the public that year. Guernsey held a contest to name the area, as he didn't like the area's nickname of Fly Camp or Camp Lincoln, which was named for popular Colton judge Amos Wayne, who frequently camped in the area and resembled the assassinated president. About 180 names were suggested, but the name Crestline won the competition. (T.)

A frequent camper in the Crest area, Dr. Wesley Thompson from Colton suggested the name Crestline in the 1906 contest. The name was not successfully used until 13 years later when, in 1919 postmaster Samuel Dillin moved the post office from Skyland Heights down to the old Arrowhead Reservoir Company's former cement warehouse building, which was vacant because there was less snow. Dillin adopted the Crestline name for the post office, and the town claimed it as well. (T.)

Samuel W. Dillin, a former Hollywood movie scriptwriter for the Keystone Cops, came to the mountains to die peacefully from what had been diagnosed as a terminal illness, which turned out to be asthma. Instead, he found the water and environment to be healthy and he lived for another 15 years. He opened a photograph shop, general store, and tavern with a dance floor in the old cement warehouse building that became the center of town. It was located at what is now the corner of Crest Forest Drive and Highway 138. (T.)

Charles S. Mann began to advertise vacation home lots around the Crest Forest and Skyland areas in the latter 1910s. The Crestline business district grew around the post office, which was next door to Dillin's Crestline Tavern. When Dillin retired as Crestline's postmaster in 1929, Mann took the position. Land subdivision was not on a massive scale, and home construction was quite different from how subdivisions are built today. (R.)

The Crestline Tavern was the former cement warehouse of the Arrowhead Reservoir Company and became the center of town, especially for publicity shots. It had character, was large, and always had significant businesses through the years, including the tavern and dance hall, the general store, a trading post, and Dillin's photography shop. Most significantly, it was the location of the first Crestline Post Office, which gave Crestline its name. It was the stage stop for the business district of Crestline. (R.)

Until the Crestline Tavern burned down in the early 1950s (it was then Cliff's Trading Post), it was the oldest building in town and stood as an anchor and symbol of the community with personality as the town grew around it. Charles S. Mann was the postmaster while also selling property in the Crestline and Skyland subdivisions. He would have stage lines bring up prospects from the valley and he made sure they always stopped to enjoy the Old Town area and atmosphere. (R.)

Garage - Crestline Village.

Office of Crestline Village.

Stage Station, Post Office & General Store, Crestline Village.

Cafe and Grocery, Crestline Village.

Pioneer Monument, Head of Old Mormon Trail, Crestline Village.

Bakery and Confectionery, Crestline Village.

Part of Business District, Crestline Village.

Business District of Crestline Village

Oil Station and Garage, Crestline Village.

Hardware and Plumbing, Crestline Village.

Native Sons Club House, Crestline Village.

Part of Business District, Crestline Village.

The Crestline business district was highly touted by Charles S. Mann as he promoted his Skyland and Crestline Village subdivisions. From one of his brochures, this shows the various businesses in town around 1927. An important feature is that the Native Sons of the Golden West already had a clubhouse in town. Crestline was considered historic from its earliest days, and residents honored their Mormon and logging heritage. (T.)

The roads were described as "improved" when bridges were constructed, however even the Rim of the World Road was only hard packed dirt (eventually oil was sprayed on it to keep down the dust) until the Rim of the World High Gear Road was finished in the 1930s. This Rim of the World Park bridge was an improvement over the creek fords that went through the washes found in some of the other areas of the mountain. (T.)

Until the Rim of the World High Gear Road was completed and for many years thereafter, most visitors came to the mountains by stage and taxi lines. The Chamberlain Motor Company charged the normal price of $1.90 for a one-way trip to the mountains. Most scheduled stage lines made three weekly round trips to the resort areas. (T.)

The Rim O' World Tavern and Inn began in the 1920s as a place for visitors to stay while enjoying the mountains and considering the purchase of their own mountain hideaway. It was located across the street, just east of the Crestline Tavern. Charles S. Mann had his sales office there. The inn had a restaurant and grocery store and the tavern featured cool drinks and billiards. Notice the fire-hose reel, as the fire department had not yet been formed. (T.)

The trees gave way as the road was paved and widened by 1948, when this photograph was taken. The tavern was very popular during the war years, as the government used the empty vacation homes in the Crestline area for off-base housing for military personnel from Norton Air Force Base in San Bernardino, just 15 miles away. The Rim O' World Tavern and Inn burned down in a spectacular fire in 1949, which, because of its location at the crest of the mountain, could be seen from as far away as Riverside. (R.)

41

There was a park between the Crestline and Rim O' World Taverns. It held a memorial cannon with a plaque honoring the exploits of the Mormon Pioneers during the early 1930s and the 1922 Mormon Road Monument (see page 13) (T.)

This view, looking west along Crest Forest Drive in the 1940s, shows the entire "Top Town" business district and in the far distance, on the left, the sign for Judge Peter Cormack's insurance business. The back of Cormack's store was used as the courthouse for many years. (Steele Photo Service.)

This aerial view shows Old Town Crestline in 1949, after the Rim O' World Tavern had burned and before the Crestline Tavern (the old cement warehouse) burned in 1951. (R.)

This 1930s photograph looks east from the location of Crest Forest Drive and Woodland in Old Town Crestline. The tree stump is now the location of the patio of a restaurant, and Roy's Texaco Garage is now an empty lot. Looking from left to right is Roy's Garage, Heaps Grocery, across the street to the right at the corner is the park, the Crestline Tavern and Post Office, Crest Forest Fire Station No. 2, Crest Cafe, and the Soda Fountain/Drug Store. (R.)

Crestline was promoted as a four-season resort for it advertised the snow as strongly as the summer season. This postcard states, "CRESTLINE VILLAGE on the Rim O' the World, San Bernardino Mountains . . . Nearest and Most Accessible of all Snow Areas . . . Convenient to all Winter Sports Events . . . Toboggans and Skis for Rent . . . Free Instruction in Cross Country Skiing by Competent Instructor . . . Learn to Ski at Crestline Village." (T.)

This view of Old Town Crestline looks east along Crest Forest Drive in February 1944. Beginning on the left is Heap's Grocery and the USO office. Across the road is the Amusements Bowling and Arcade, which is next to Weber's One Stop Shop (under all the snow). Across the street on the far right is the Rim of the World Tavern and the Union Gas Station. The drugstore sign hides the other businesses. (R.)

44

This is the corner of Highway 138 and Crest Forest Drive during the 1944 snowstorm. Murphy's Dance Hall often had Ozzie Nelson's Band providing music during the war years. Next door, Cliff's Trading Post sold jewelry, clothing, gifts, and most items a person might need except for food (Weber's and Heaps Markets were across the street). (R.)

Weber's One Stop Store believed they sold every item a person should need, including ice for the many ice boxes in town. During the summer, they sold ice cream from the front counter. This store was directly across the street from the Rim O' World Tavern and Inn. The Weber's sons moved to Los Angeles and began the Weber's Bread Bakery Company. The porch has been enclosed and the gas pump removed, but the building is still recognizable and now houses Hilltop Liquor. (R.)

As the years progressed, Charles S. Mann continued to develop more areas for housing and vacation cabins. This unique house that he advertised on so many of his brochures is now the Presbyterian Church preschool building. (T.)

Charles S. Mann expanded the housing district and built an amphitheater at the eastern end of his property. When Lake Gregory was built in 1938, some businessmen began to open and expand the business district along Huston Flat Road (now Lake Drive) to benefit visitors to the lake. This is Huston Flat Road at 1000-Pines, around 1950. From left to right, the businesses are Fountain Grill/Malts Goodwin's and Sons Market, Rogers Fountain, and Lee's Bicycle Rental, which had bikes available for 50¢ an hour. (R.)

This is Huston Flat Road, looking west. On the left is Goodwin's and Sons Market (where Lake Drive Hardware is now located) and the Stockade Cafe, with the upright log facade. Sledding along the street was a popular adventure during snowstorms in the days before too many cars populated the area. A lookout at the top and bottom of the street secured it as a toboggan or sled run. (GC.)

The Pilands, who formerly operated the Yodeler restaurant for the Club San Moritz, pose in front of the Stockade Cafe they built, showing off the rustic exterior. It was built to look like an old fort or western stockade from the frontier days and was thus given its name. It was located across the street from the Frontier Arcade, which is now the garden center for Ace Hardware. (GC.)

A few years later, Goodwin's Market built a new modern supermarket and moved across Wildrose on Lake Drive to a new location, where Crestline's main post office is now located. Lake Drive Hardware then opened in Goodwin's former location. Though this photograph is from the 1960s, not much has changed since then except the style of the cars. (T.)

Located on Lake Drive was the American National Bank. The building began as a real estate office for the Club San Moritz. (T.)

This is the corner of Lake Drive and Lake Gregory Drive, looking towards Lake Gregory, in 1968. Notice there is no stop sign, as this corner did not have much traffic. The grading is for an Arco gasoline station built there that later became an equipment rental yard before being replaced by a 7-11. Across the street, to the right, is where Goodwin's Market is currently located. It had a small real estate office for the properties of the Club San Moritz at this time (notice that the lake even looks different). This was in the days before the regional park took control of the lake. (T.)

Jamboree Days developed from many sources. The Fourth of July holiday has been celebrated in the mountains with barbeques and large parties since the 1880s sawmill days. The Crest Forest/Crestline Resorts Chamber of Commerce capitalized upon the natural desire for people to visit the mountains to escape the heat by developing Jamboree Days in the 1970s. Previous celebrations have been called Sawmill Days, Alpine Days, and Jamboree Daze. This 1968 photograph shows front-row flag carriers Ted Dewar (left) and Art Blum from the Skyforest Elks leading the parade down Lake Drive past Manzanita Drive. (R.)

A. G. Hamilton and Arthur Gregory dammed Dart Creek, creating Moon Lake, and built a private club in the Valley of the Moon in 1923. The Arrowhead Valley Club members were also affiliated with Masonic organizations, so the streets have names like Temple and Pyramid. The surrounding property was subdivided for club members to purchase. (R.)

The Arrowhead Valley Club was quite successful. Moon Lake was only six feet deep and froze most winters. It was used for fishing, canoeing, and ice skating. Access by auto stage to the area was up Arrowhead Road, past Pinecrest Resort (Twin Peaks), and down the old Arosa logging road to Arrowhead Valley. (R.)

The Arrowhead Valley Club was quite prestigious and had many prominent members. The Depression hit the club hard and plans for expansion were cancelled and it subsequently closed. The building sat out those years as a boarding house run by the Threat family as the former clubhouse was the largest building in the area. This is the winter of 1933 in the Valley of the Moon. (R.)

The 1932 Chamber of Commerce 49er Days, held at Arthur Gregory's Thousand Pines Camp, was very successful at bringing in tourists to spend money. Both locals and vacationers enjoyed the end-of-summer event. (T.)

The chamber's 1933 fourth annual event was to recreate an 1849-style, gold-mining town named Paradise Gulch, with townsfolk wearing 49er Days costumes and adopting characters based on the story "The Luck of Roaring Camp," in the Valley of the Moon. Unfortunately, due to the repeal of Prohibition and the availability of legal booze and too much gambling on the boxing match between the CCC Camps, a riot broke out. This is the script issued by the Snow Bank for items for 49er Days. (T.)

The Arrowhead Valley Club building was purchased in 1939 and the Club San Moritz was established, as the completion of Lake Gregory, in 1938, attracted new interest in the area. The building was remodeled and upgraded inside and out. The new, exclusive private club became very popular and made Valley of the Moon a center of activity, changing the name to Switzerland.

52

The Seely Flat area (now known as the Valley of Enchantment) was the location of the first mountain sawmill. It was built in 1853 by brothers David and Wellington Seely along Seely Creek at the current location of Camp Seeley. Seely Flat was popular for sawmills, with as many as four to five in operation at various times, including this one cutting different tree types simultaneously. For 50 years, until the national forest was established, Seely Flat was actively logged, but never clear-cut. (T.)

Byron Waters, a successful San Bernardino lawyer, bought Seely Flat in 1895. He was elected to the state assembly in 1877 and represented San Bernardino County during the drafting of the California State Constitution. He planted apple trees in the sawed-over area of Seely Flat, as had lumberman La Praix years before. The Waters family owned the land between Camp Seeley and the Tetley's Valley of Enchantment subdivision until 1945, when they sold to the Club San Moritz for the Pitch and Putt Golf Center, which was later turned into a mobile-home park. (T.)

SUMMER —— CAMP SEELEY —— WINTER

FOR many years a popular summer vacation camp, Seeley now offers itself to the public as the first all-year around municipal mountain playground of the City of Los Angeles.

EVERY summer, thousands of persons have been accustomed to spending their vacations in this beautiful recreation area maintained by the City of Los Angeles for public use.

Summer Activities

In summer Camp Seeley is a cool and delightful mountain retreat, an ideal vacation spot. For those who wish to rest, the rustic camp in the shadow of great pines and oaks and cedars is a quiet haven. For those who enjoy an active vacation, there are opportunities for almost every kind of mountain recreation.

Now popular demand has caused the Playground and Recreational Department of Los Angeles to transform Camp Seeley into a mountain playground whose recreational advantages are open to the public at all seasons of the year.

Winter Activities

In winter Camp Seeley is a popular rendezvous for those who like to play in the snow. Winter sports are then the center of attraction at Seeley municipal mountain playground, and innumerable activities radiate out from the recreational lodge with its great fireplace and roaring fire.

HIKING
HORSEBACK RIDING
SWIMMING
TENNIS
BASEBALL
CROQUET
VOLLEYBALL
RECREATIONAL LODGE

TOBOGGANING
SLEDDING
SKIING
SNOWSHOE TRIPS
SNOW SPORTS
RECREATIONAL LODGE

Camp Seeley was started in 1914 when the city of Los Angeles decided it needed a campground for its citizens and employees to visit, copying New York City, which opened camps in upstate New York during the same era. The city purchased the former site of the Seely Sawmill. (T.)

John Adams, a direct descendant of Pres. John Quincy Adams, came to the mountains in 1919 and changed the town. He owned the first gas station and started the first phone system (a party line), which stretched from Twin Peaks to Cedarpines Park, with all 19 families connected by wire. His wife, Ida Mae, operated the switchboard from their home. Adams built many rock walls and chimneys for cabins in the growing Crestline community. The couple were the cooks at Camp Seeley for many years. (T.)

Rim of the World Park

SITUATED

Thirteen miles from San Bernardino adjoining Camp Seeley, Los Angeles City all year playground. Motor Transit stages daily to the Lodge.

New high-gear road makes an easy grade all of the way to the land, with paved highway.

Byron Waters was going blind and in 1924 sold most of his homestead land to Frank Tetley Sr., who developed it as Rim of the World Park. He named it after the highway to capitalize on its widespread fame, although the road was miles away from the subdivision. As a state highway commissioner, Tetley cut the ribbon on the Rim of the World High Gear Road in 1932. The name of the subdivision was changed to the Valley of Enchantment several years later. (T.)

Tetley put in waterlines, electricity, and roads to reach the lots. As the property sold, he would develop more land and added annexes. The Valley of Enchantment Mutual Water Company is still owned by the property owners and operates today. Here are Tetley and his son Frank Jr. watching the waterlines being installed. (T.)

Like most developers of the era, Tetley sold his property by many means, including barbeques on-site. He also brought bags of apples from the property down to his businesses in Riverside to entice buyers, as well as having four diorama-type paintings of the property on the walls of his hotel in Riverside. Here is a baseball game being played next to the Rim of the World Park clubhouse. (T.)

In 1928, Los Angeles Municipal Mountain Playground at Camp Seeley sponsored a winter carnival, which brought 30,000 people to Seely Flat. Some of the winter activities included ice hockey, ice skating, sledding, tobogganing, and a 1920s favorite—snowshoeing.

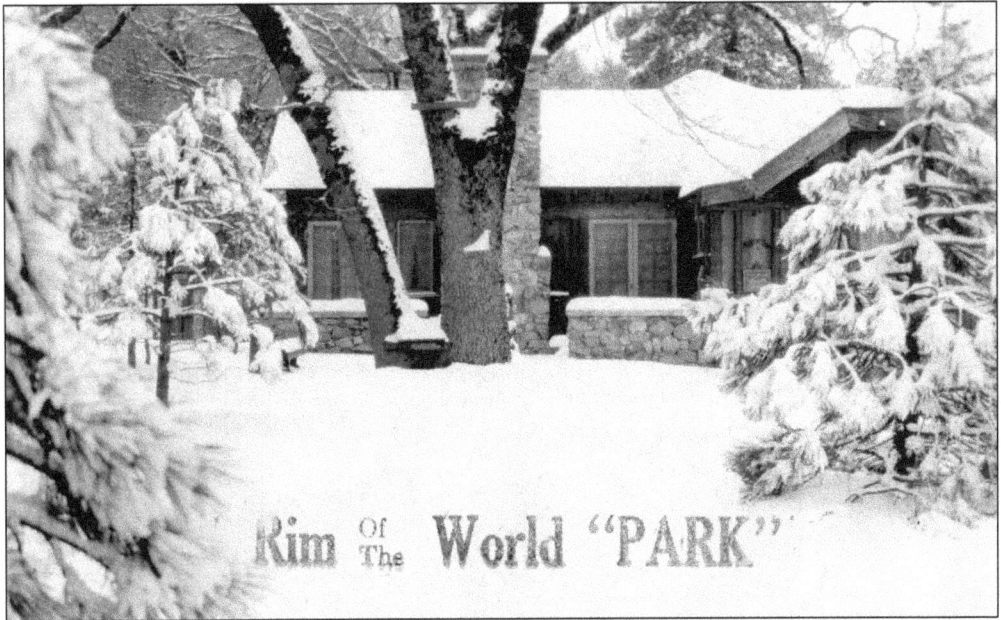

Rim Of The World "PARK"

Tetley's vacation home (shown here) was typical of the rustic construction of the era. It was also his real estate office. Because he was well-funded, Tetley was able to get through the Depression without the bank foreclosing on the development. Not all of Crestline's developments were as fortunate. Of the 1,500 water shares in the Valley of Enchantment Mutual Water Company available by 1934, over 1,100 were sold. (T.)

Most purchasers of property in the 1920s built their own cabins. Whole families made weekly trips during the summer months, bringing supplies and camping equipment to the cabin site while constructing their vacation homes. Because of the families' personal involvement, Crestline has many cabins that have been owned by several generations of the same family. (T.)

The Barn was obviously originally a barn used for oxen and horses from the earliest times. It is said Job the ox (of Job's Peak fame) used to sleep there. It's known that Byron Waters used it as a stable for his horses. From the 1930s to the 1960s, it was the community center for the area. The Crashline Players, a local theater company, performed its plays there. It had a bar, a dance floor, and an old logging wagon hanging from the ceiling for decoration. It is now being used as a church. (T.)

The Valley of Enchantment was very proud of its cement community swimming pool. It did cause controversy during one year of drought during the 1930s, as the shareholders of the mutual water company debated whether to fill it for the summer season since water was so scarce and the wells were running low. As the years progressed, the trampolines for the Frontier Arcade were built over the hole from the swimming pool. (T.)

Horseback riding was a popular activity since the forest was so close and had numerous riding trails. Horses could be rented or boarded at the stables next to Camp Seeley. Barbara Rovira raised champion Morgan horses and ran the Plush Paddock, a dinner house and bar at Rancho Rovira. (T.)

As the population of Valley of Enchantment grew, the business district expanded. In addition to Johnnies Market, there were three restaurants, J&W Machine Shop, the Barn, real estate offices, Frontier Arcade and miniature golf course, V.O.E. Lumber Company, Smith's Drilling, the water company, a Shell gas station, the V.O.E. Stables, and the Plush Paddock Lounge and dinner house. In the 1950s, the Valley of Enchantment was referred to as "V.O.E., the Valley of Everything." (T.)

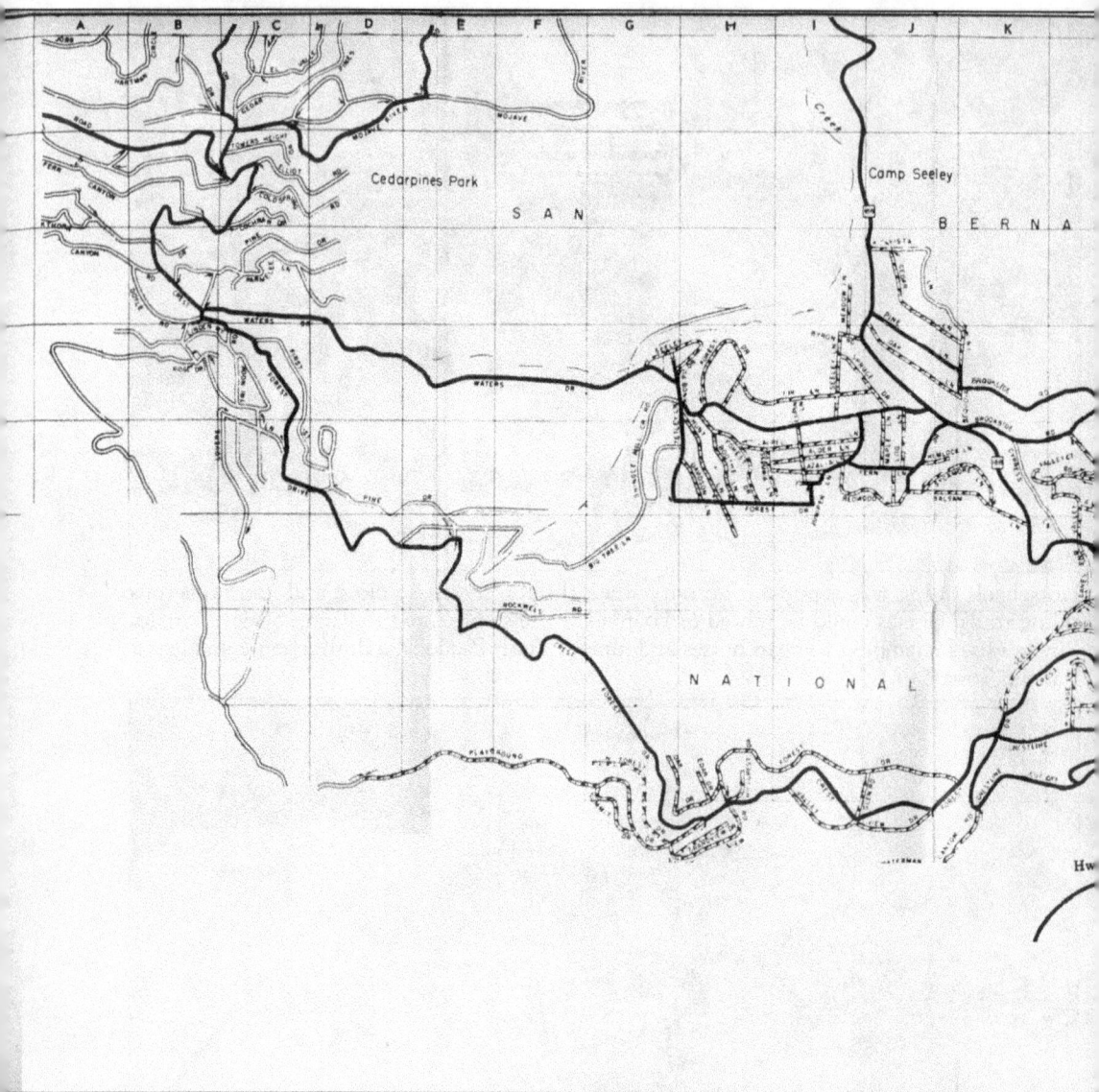

This 1965 map of the greater Crestline area shows the locations of the various subdivisions and roads. It's interesting to note that Straightway is only straight for five blocks. Huston Flat Road from Old Town to Lake Gregory is now known as Lake Drive. Seeley Flat Road from uptown Crestline to the Valley of Enchantment is now Highway 138. Crest Forest Road was the route of

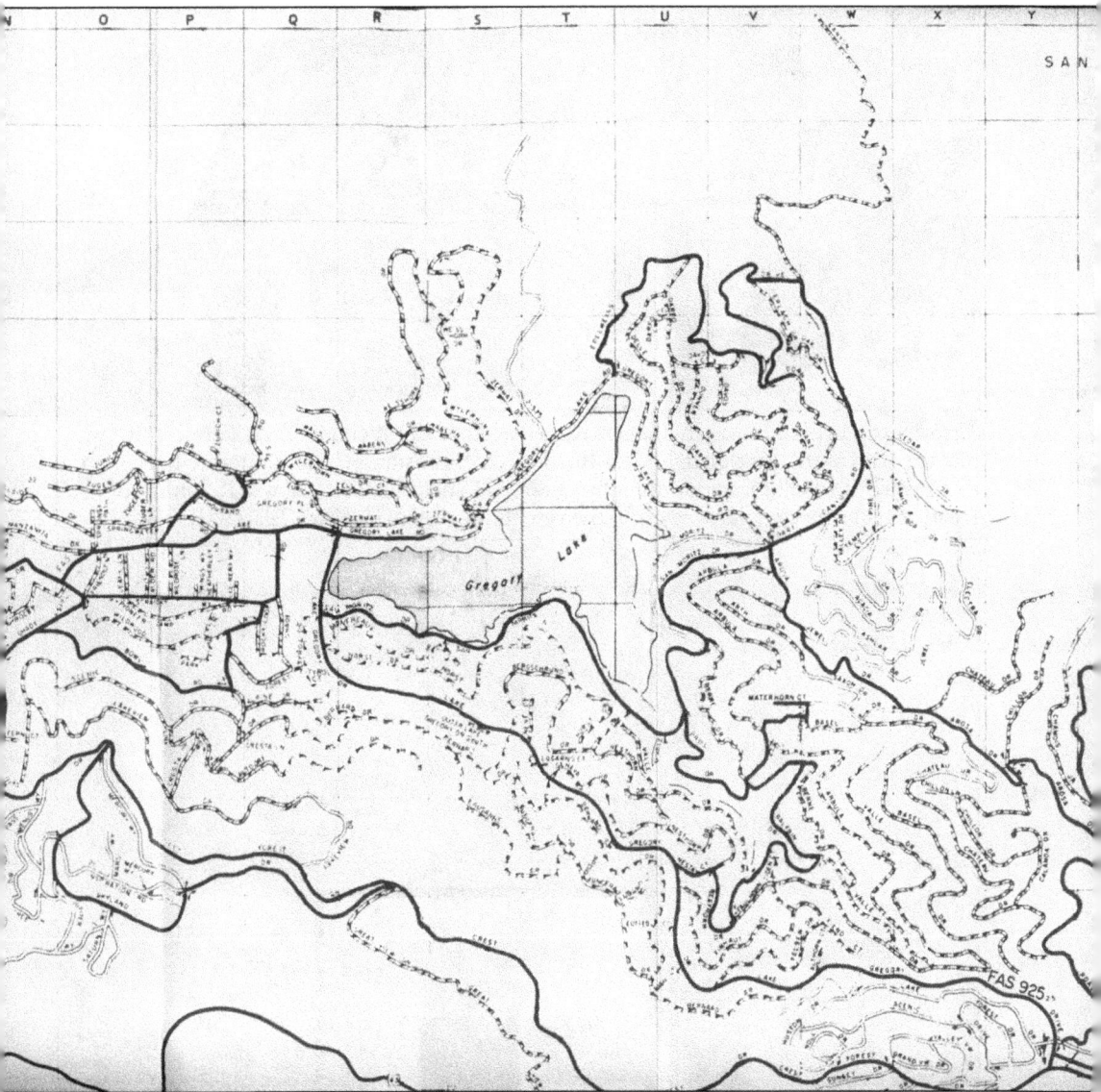

the Rim of the World Road before the High Gear Road was built to bypass Crestline. Highway 138 to Highway 18 was the road built in 1932 to connect to the High Gear Road. The original route into the Valley of the Moon was from Twin Peaks and down the old logging road, using Arosa Drive as access for the Arrowhead Valley Club.

Arrowhead Highlands was an area developed at the eastern end of Crest Forest Drive where it met the Rim of the World High Gear Road. A cafe, gas station, and store were built there next to a distinctive rock formation (used frequently in silent movies) known as Sphinx Rock. The location had a spectacular view from the rim all the way to Catalina Island. (R.)

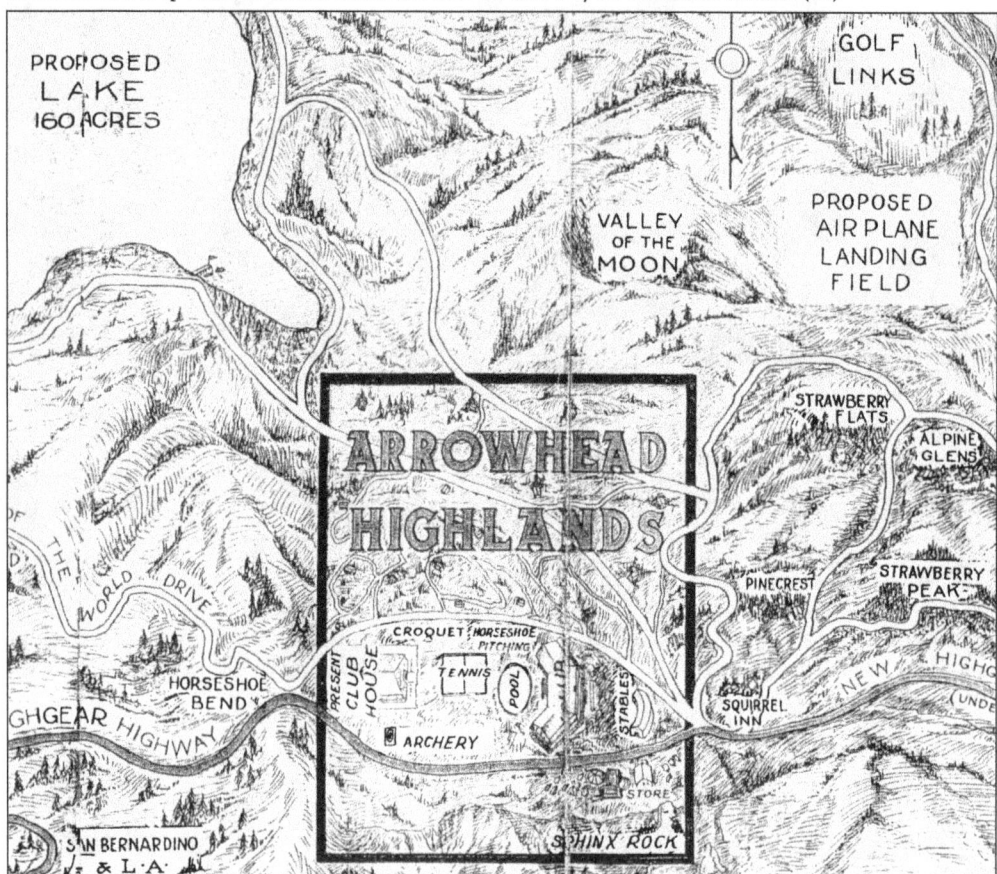

This is a map of Arrowhead Highlands as described in a brochure. It had grandiose plans and was well situated, but the Depression greatly affected the subdivision. Some of the community buildings on the map were never completed. Many land subdivisions and resorts used maps as excellent promotional tools. (R.)

Arrowhead Highlands subdivision was under-funded and never successfully developed into the dreams of its owners, however Lee's Garage was successful and the cafe eventually was turned into the Cliffhanger Restaurant, famous for its views of the entire inland empire and out to the Pacific Ocean. This view is from their advertising brochure.

Located on Highway 18 at the east end of the Narrows section (that ran below and south of Skyland, Horseshoe Bend, and Arrowhead Highlands), the Arrowhead Highlands Gas Station closed in the 1960s, and then the restaurant in 2003 (just before the Old Fire). Continuing rock slides have kept the Narrows section of Highway 18 closed many months of the year, forcing traffic to detour through the town of Crestline and return to the highway at Arrowhead Highlands. (R.)

One of the oldest sections of Crestline, just east of Skyland and west of Arrowhead Highlands and located along the rim, is Horseshoe Bend. Shown here is their community park with basketball and volleyball courts and hiking trails. The homeowners association (Horseshoe Bend Mountain Club Incorporated) began in 1909 and is still active. (T.)

Horseshoe Bend was greatly affected by the 2003 Old Fire, with numerous cabins along the mountaintop crest having been burned. The firefighters were able to stop the fire there and save the rest of the Crestline community from the raging inferno. Other areas of Crestline were developed later as housing, such as Brookside, Dart Canyon, and Mile High Park, but not as resorts, so they did not have the lodge or clubhouse buildings, community centers, or water companies, and organized activities as early developments like Valley View Park, Crestline, Valley of the Moon, and Cedar Pines Park did. (T.)

Three

LAKE GREGORY

In 1892, the Little Bear Reservoir (Lake Arrowhead) project was originally developed as a massive multi-lake project. The intention of the Little Bear Reservoir Company was to capture the water from seven watershed areas of the San Bernardino Mountains and divert it from its natural flow to the desert to the San Bernardino Valley to irrigate crops and orchards. The company was inspired by the Big Bear Dam project that supplied a steady, year-round water supply for Redlands citrus growers. One of the proposed locations for a lake was in Huston Flat (current location of Lake Gregory), where a tunnel was dug toward the project under the engineering skills of Fred T. Perris. Before it could be completed, the Little Bear Reservoir Project was deemed unlawful, as the water could not legally be diverted from one watershed to another for irrigation purposes. The tunnel was abandoned, as was the idea for a lake in Huston Flat. This is how Huston Flat appeared in 1900.

ORANGE Blossom Brand

GROWN AND PACKED BY A. GREGORY AT REDLANDS, SAN BERNARDINO COUNTY, CALIFOR[NIA]

As Crestline became a thriving village in the 1930s, Arthur Gregory was a Redlands citrus grower who owned a sawmill (Gregory had developed the Valley of the Moon area in the 1920s). His mill was cutting wood for his Orange Blossom Brand citrus boxes and he began pushing for a lake in the Huston Flat area. It would supply water for the Crest Forest Fire District, lessen the demand on local wells, and could provide recreational activities like those being enjoyed at Lake Arrowhead. Gregory owned much of the Huston Flat area. (T.)

Arthur Gregory formed the Crest Forest Water District in 1936 to provide water for the areas of the Valley of the Moon, the future San Moritz area, Thousand Pines, and Arrowhead Highlands. A $25,000 tax bond was passed by 32 voters in the district to pay for stage one of the construction of a dam to create Lake Gregory. (T.)

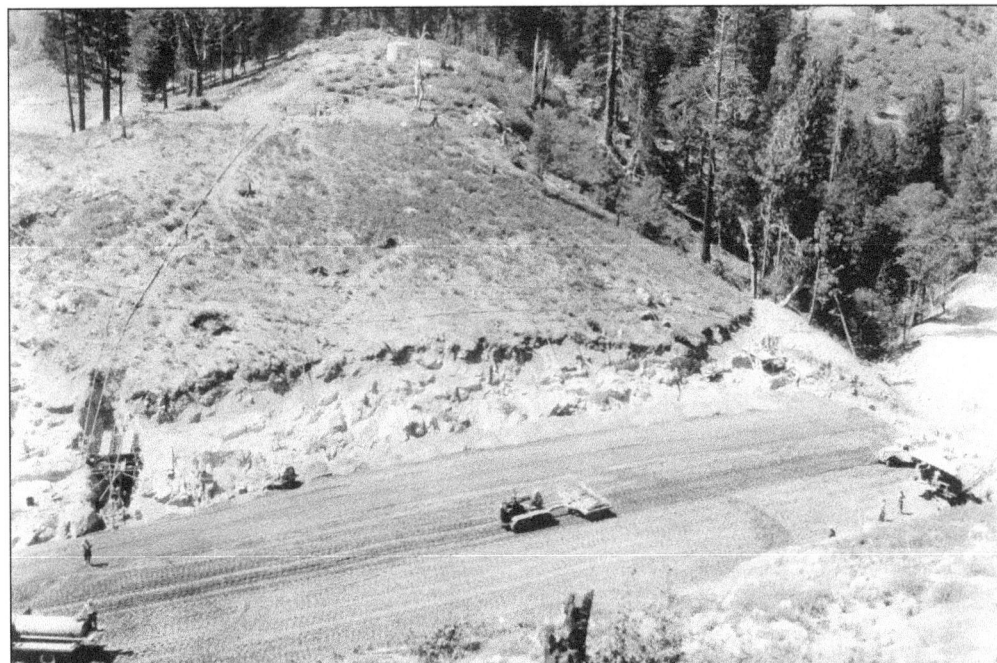

There was some controversy over the water district, as non-resident landowners worried their taxes would become too expensive, so the areas of Crestline Village, Cedar Pines Park, the Valley of Enchantment, and Skyland were excluded from the water district. Later on, during construction, developer Charles S. Mann and Judge Peter Cormack from Crestline supported completion of the project. (S.)

The Lake Gregory Dam project was federally funded under the Works Progress Administration (WPA), which supplied some of the manpower and paid workers 40¢ an hour. The workers who did not live in Crestline were housed at Gregory's Thousand Pines Camp. The WPA funds ran out before completion in July 1937. The Crestline community then financially supported the project and the dam (shown) was almost completed by the March 1938 flood. (R.)

The deluge of March 1938 flooded many areas of Southern California. Because the Lake Gregory Dam was 95 percent complete, the lake filled in three days and saved the Las Flores Ranch in Summit Valley from destructive flooding. The lake level was lowered to remove equipment and complete the finishing touches. An island was revealed when the lake level was lowered in May 1938. (T.)

This is Lake Gregory in 1938. Arthur Gregory designed a 150-foot "reserve strip" around the lake to guarantee public access to the shore and to prevent private homes from being built on the lakeshore. This is the area that today constitutes San Bernardino County's Regional Park at Lake Gregory. (T.)

Lake Gregory became the public tourist attraction and water supply that Arthur Gregory envisioned. The San Moritz Land and Water Company purchased most of the land around the lake, beyond the reserve strip, to sell for vacation housing. Only members of Club San Moritz could purchase those lots and homes.

A horse trail was constructed around the lake and stables rented horses to the tourists. Sand was brought to the Lake Gregory Public Beach in the early 1950s in dump trucks from Mentone. Many vacationers came to Crestline to enjoy the lake, the wonderful cool summer breezes, and the smell of pine trees in the clear mountain air. Motels opened around town, real estate became a going business, and families would come yearly to visit the area.

In the 1970s, after Club San Moritz closed, San Bernardino County purchased the lake and the reserve strip around it and developed the new Lake Gregory Regional Park. The county has added a waterslide and has horseshoe pits, rental boats, and paddle boards available, as well as a family picnic area in the park.

Known as Leisure Shores, the clubhouse of the Crest Forest Senior Citizens Club, Inc. was developed from the old teen center and bathhouse of the Club San Moritz. The teen center is pictured at right (after it was flooded in the 1970s) and on page 81 (during its heyday in the 1960s). The senior citizens club currently leases Leisure Shores from the County of San Bernardino, as the building is located in the County Regional Park on the shore of Lake Gregory. The dry creek next to the structure sometimes becomes a raging torrent, and members of the club spent the summer of 2005 renovating after a winter flood washed it out. The center photograph, taken in the 1970s, shows the seniors replacing the roof of the washed-out teen center during its conversion into Leisure Shores. The photograph below shows the club as seen from a boat on the lake. The very active group of seniors also run the Crest Forest Senior Citizens Thrift Shop in Old Town Crestline. (Above photograph S; below photograph R.)

"During"

Lake Gregory Regional Park has hosted fireworks over the lake for most Fourth of July celebrations. Crestline has sponsored Jamboree Days, with parades, floats, and youth groups involved in a local hometown-style parade. Following an extended drought and subsequent bark beetle invasion, the fireworks were put on hold for three years. Fireworks returned to Lake Gregory during the 2005 Fourth of July weekend. (A.)

This is Lake Gregory's public beach in the 1960s. The lake, which flooded the old Huston Flat sawmill area, was built in 1937 as a WPA Project. It cost $165,000 and was named after Redlands citrus grower Arthur Gregory, who was instrumental in getting federal financing for the project. Many people think the public beach is special because of the trees located on the beach. (T.)

Four

CLUB SAN MORITZ

In 1938, as the Depression was waning, Club San Moritz was formed. The clubhouse of the former Arrowhead Valley Club, adjacent to Moon Lake, was modernized, with the exterior remodeled to a more alpine look than its previous rustic appearance. Club San Moritz was established "to promote art, amusements and entertainment; to provide Club accommodations; to promote physical and social welfare of members and their families and guests; to bring together, unite and cement friendships; and fraternal association among such people as may be admitted to membership therein." (T.)

The dances were a way to enjoy the club and encourage new members to join. The land around Lake Gregory was purchased by the San Moritz Land and Water Company and sold as vacation homes for Club San Moritz members. You had to qualify as a member before you could purchase property in the San Moritz area. (R.)

The Moon Lake Post Office, operated by Fritz Mueller, changed its name to "Switzerland" to match the San Moritz theme of the area. Shown is Anita Piland, daughter of Lil and Newt Piland, who operated the restaurant at the Club San Moritz in Valley of the Moon. The Pilands also built and ran the exclusive Club San Moritz Supper Club, Chateau Cafe Piland, the Stockade, and the Yodeler at the corner of Arosa and Dart Canyon Road. (S.; R.)

The clubhouse was fully remodeled in 1939 using an alpine theme. Activities at the club included dining (with great chefs), dancing, canoeing, hiking, tennis, horseback riding, fishing, nature walks, socializing, and meeting others with similar interests. (S.)

Winter activities at Club San Moritz included snow shoeing, tobogganing, and ice skating—quite a nice diversion from the sunny, warm weather Southern California experiences year round in the valley. (R.)

This is Club San Moritz, with canoes on Moon Lake, in the Valley of the Moon. Rowing canoes on the lake and fishing were popular weekend activities during the summer months. As the 1940s progressed, more club members began to use Lake Gregory. They set up boat docks and held fishing derbies there. (T.)

After World War II, club membership grew as many people were moving to California and the demand for recreation was increasing. "The best private club in the world" was a comment often heard from its members. Club San Moritz decided to lease seven-and-a-half acres on the shore of Lake Gregory to expand their facilities. Unfortunately, before the new lodge building was completed, the old clubhouse burned. (T.)

LAKE GREGORY

SCALE

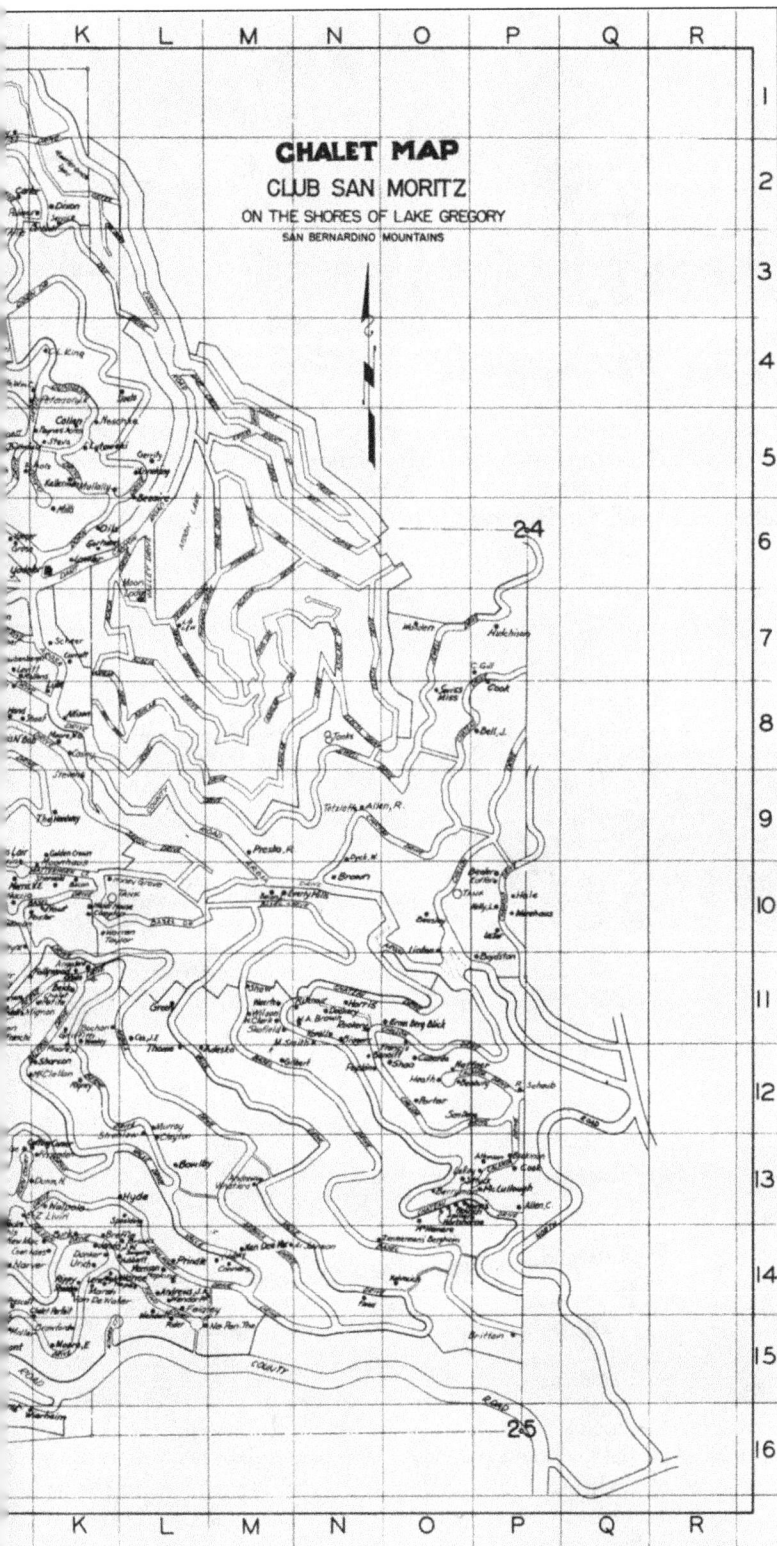

CHALET MAP
CLUB SAN MORITZ
ON THE SHORES OF LAKE GREGORY
SAN BERNARDINO MOUNTAINS

Club San Moritz published maps to the chalets at least once a year in *The Yodeler*, a magazine printed monthly for club members. The magazine changed size and improved in quality as the years progressed. *The Yodeler* told of monthly events, holiday activities, encouraged new memberships, and advertised chalets for rent. This is a 1970s map of all the subdivisions the Club San Moritz built. (T.)

The new clubhouse, located on the shores of Lake Gregory, was completed in the early 1950s and offered more activities, a modern facility, and was closer to most of the chalets. The seven-and-a-half acres of grounds had immaculate gardens and a teen center, beach, ice skating rink, and canals. The restaurant had excellent chefs and Sunday morning buffets were said to be delicious. (T.)

Club San Moritz had its own private docks for boats, a private beach, and canals that could be paddled through where the baseball field is now located. As members retired from their "down the hill jobs," they often moved to their mountain chalet. Teens met other teens in the safe environment of Club San Moritz and many lifelong friendships were made. The Club San Moritz was a lifestyle of its own to many of its members. (T.)

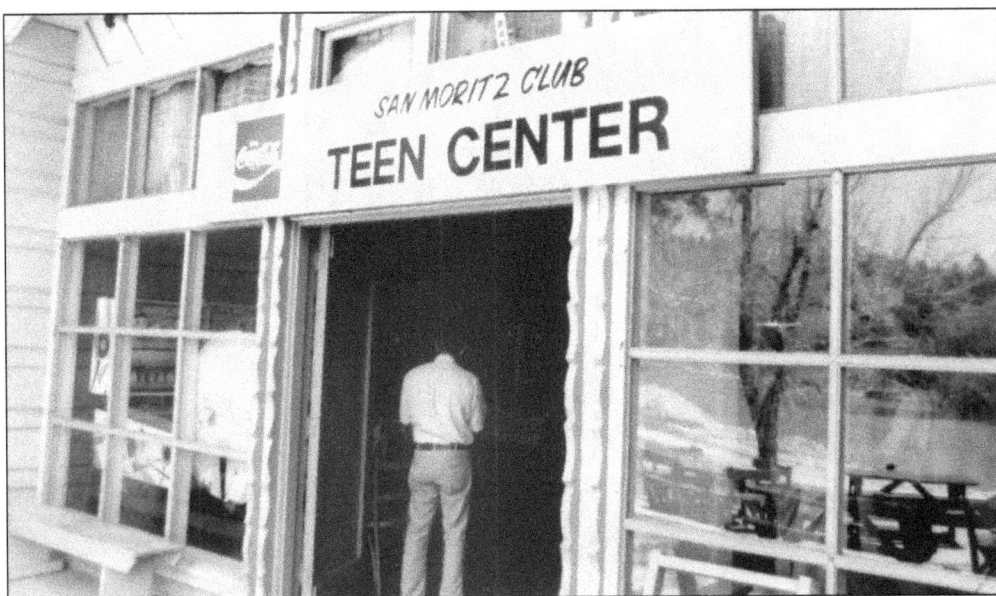

There was a teen center, where dances were held in the main lodge, an ice-skating facility, and a teen beach at Club San Moritz. Activities for all ages of family members were included with the membership price. The teen center was restored after it was flooded out in the 1970s and is now the Crest Forest Senior Citizens Center, known as "Leisure Shores." (S.)

The Club San Moritz indoor ice-skating rink collapsed under the weight of snow one Christmas day, and the club constructed a new building and ice rink. When the club closed, the building was sold to a manufacturing company and moved to the top of Waterman Canyon, at the interchange with Highway 18. Unfortunately, it burned to the ground during the 2003 Old Fire. (S.)

This is a typical page from *The Yodeler* magazine, showing the members enjoying the many activities at Club San Moritz. (T.)

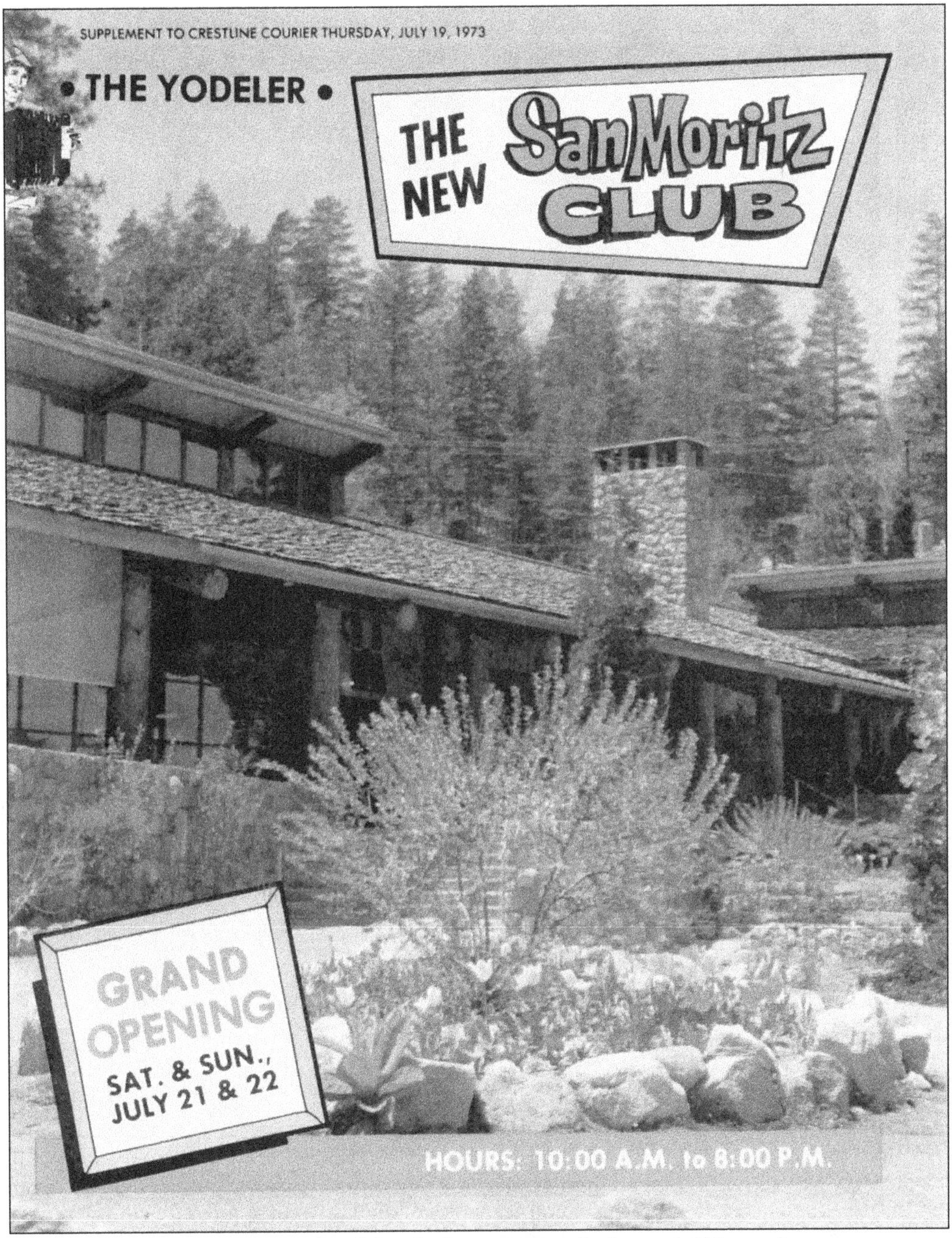

SUPPLEMENT TO CRESTLINE COURIER THURSDAY, JULY 19, 1973
• THE YODELER •
THE NEW San Moritz CLUB
GRAND OPENING
SAT. & SUN., JULY 21 & 22
HOURS: 10:00 A.M. to 8:00 P.M.

In 1972, one attempt to revive the club, which at one time had over 1,000 members, was to name it the San Moritz Club. The beach was always very popular with local teens. (T.)

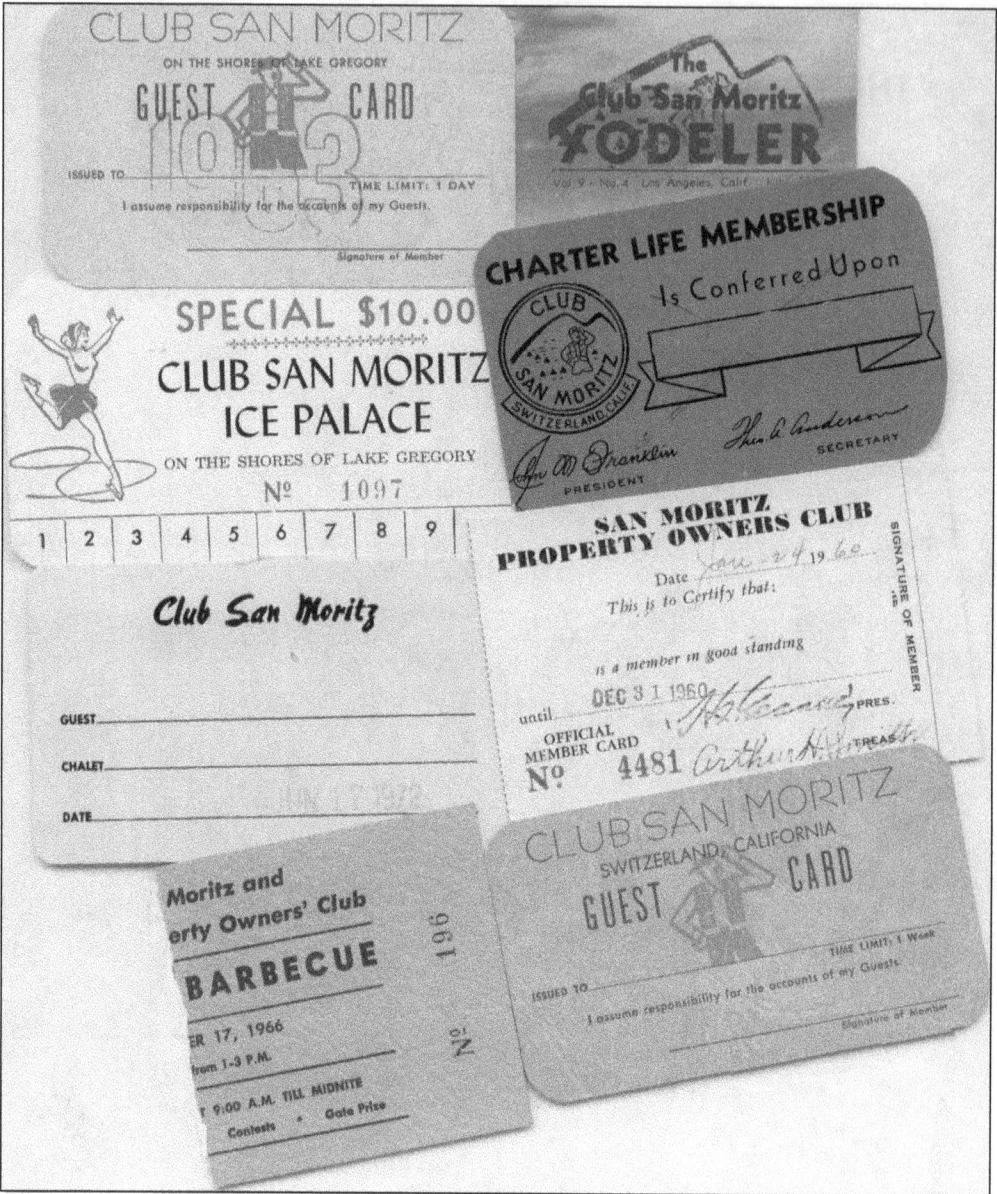

The final revival effort was the attempted organization of the San Moritz Lodge. Not enough people joined and by then the buildings were falling into disrepair. Eventually, following several owners, the county received possession of the land and buildings. The lodge building became a part of the facilities at Lake Gregory Regional Park. These are some of the membership cards issued by the Club San Moritz that became useless when it closed. (S; T.)

The seven-and-a-half acres of land that had been leased and improved by the San Moritz Club are now part of Lake Gregory Regional Park and are maintained by the county. The lodge building is available for rent, the canals have been turned into a community baseball field, and the former teen beach is popular with fishermen and those who love to feed the ducks. The gardens, though just a glimmer of their past beauty, still bloom yearly. (T.)

One of the features of the club most missed by members and the citizens of the community was the restaurant. They hired some of Southern California's best chefs and members often invited non-members in to eat and drink at the beautiful lake view restaurant and bar. (T.)

Club San Moritz had its own private beach on seven-and-a-half acres of Lake Gregory lakeshore property. This is the Children's Beach, showing the playground equipment. Parents could relax and know their children were safe while visiting Club San Moritz. (T.)

The Switzerland Monuments were originally an advertising gimmick of Club San Moritz. They were on Huston Flat Road at the entrance to the subdivision, next to their Lake Gregory Real estate office. When entering the San Moritz area, it said "Switzerland" and when leaving it said "Happy Return." Notice that the lake can be seen just behind the monuments. (R; Don Foster.)

Five

CEDAR PINES PARK

Cedar Pines Park (later changed to Cedarpines Park) is located three miles west of the community of Crestline. The Mojave Indian Trail went through the area and was used as a trade route from the desert to the ocean for hundreds of years before the Spanish arrived. Fr. Francisco Garces and Jedediah Strong Smith both saw the ocean for the first time in their long journeys from a place now identified as Monument Peak in Cedarpines Park. The Cedarpines Park (CPP) area was used by Juan Bandini for cutting logs for the Spanish-era adobe homes in the valley. They used a sawpit to cut the logs, with one man on top of the log and another in the sawpit, moving the length of the secured log while trimming it—thus the name for the area. The lumber-mill era continued as the American lumbermen came into the area and began to cut the trees. They built lumber roads in the 1870s along the old Indian trails of Sawpit and Devil's Canyon after the Mormon Lumber Road through Waterman Canyon was washed out. The subdivision era and the arrival of Prince Mozumdar added excitement to what many now consider a quiet hamlet community. (T.)

These children, including Lural Schafer, hiked from Camp Seeley, where they were camping in 1921, to the old abandoned sawmill located at Job's Peak, several miles away. Job's Peak was located at the highest point in Cedarpines Park and was named for an ox from the David Seely sawmill that enjoyed spending his grazing time chewing on the grasses on the top of the mountain. This sawmill was in operation for approximately 40 years after the Seely Mill closed. (S.)

The Patterson and Dillin Sawmill sold 760 acres in 1922 to Anloff and Houlette, who developed Cedar Pines Park. With Devil's Canyon Road as a direct route up from the valley, Cedarpines Park became an upscale development with a golf course, tennis courts, dance pavilion, a park with a swimming pool, and a general store with a post office. The community advertised hiking, hunting, fishing, and horseback riding. (R.)

The U.S. post office tightened up the name Cedar Pines Park to create the name Cedarpines Park, which has become the accepted spelling of the area, although the abbreviation remains CPP. Frank Nardi opened the community's post office in his general store and was its postmaster from 1927 to 1946. The post office eventually served over 500 homes. (R.)

Prince Mozumdar, a spiritual Christian leader from India who combined concepts of Hinduism and Buddhism to Christianity, came to the Cedarpines Park area in the 1930s and decided to build a religious retreat overlooking the desert for his followers. He purchased land and built the Pillars of God Amphitheater (above) and the Temple of Christ (below). Mozumdar built a lodge for his followers to stay in so they could study his principles while there. He conducted Sunday services and wrote over 30 books on how to live happy, fulfilling, and satisfying lives. (R.)

Prince Mozumdar operated his retreat in Cedarpines Park from the 1930s to the 1950s. He was considered a gentleman and had a charismatic personality. He converted to Christianity after years of study and combined those beliefs with spiritual truths of Buddhism and Hinduism. His books and lectures were very popular. He established the "Messianic World" to spread his message. (T.)

Upon his death in the 1950s, Prince Mozumdar donated his temple and lands to the YMCA, which used the property until the 1980s as a summer camp for children. The YMCA then sold the property to Rev. Sun Myung Moon's Unification Church. (R.)

Cedar Pines Park

A page from Cedar Pines Park's advertising brochure makes the area seem extremely appealing. Picture here are open, forested spaces, cabins, the golf course (the only one on the mountain at the time), and the plunge. The first Catholic church in the area was formed and met at Joe Bertucci's General Store and Dance Hall in the 1940s until the St. Francis X. Cabrini Catholic Church was completed. (T.)

One of the first three stations of the volunteer Crest Forest Fire District was located in Cedar Pines Park in 1929. The station can be seen on the right of this 1950 photograph and in the center is the Cedar Pines Park Market and Bertucci's Hayloft Restaurant. On the far left is the Cedarpines Danceland Cafe building. (T.)

Six

Towns near Crestline

Rimforest is a town five miles directly east of Crestline on the Rim of the World Highway (State Highway 18). Rimforest is directly located on the highway and the 101-mile marker, where the Rim of the World Road was dedicated just west of town. The community has suffered from numerous fires and landslides over the years, but the views all the way to Perris Valley, downtown Los Angeles, and Catalina Island in the Pacific Ocean have attracted artists and other creative people to the area.

Pinecrest Resort

Twin Peaks was formerly known as both Alpine and Strawberry Flats and is located four miles east of Crestline. The community grew up near Dr. John Baylis's Pinecrest Resort (shown) and the private Squirrel Inn Club. Both are located on the road to Lake Arrowhead and part of the Crest Forest Fire District centered in Crestline. (T.)

On the road to Lake Arrowhead, Twin Peaks is the highest elevation of the western San Bernardino Mountain towns. The name was chosen because the post-office name of Strawberry was already taken by a town in Yuba County. Well known, Twin Peaks postmasters included the Dexters (1918), Sara and Bert Switzer (1919–1940), and Lela Spindler (1975). (T.)

94

The county building at Twin Peaks is located on the old Strawberry Flat Campground site. The Dexter family built a sawmill, a resort, and many of the structures in the area. Julia and Gregg Dexter's resort, the Alpine Terrace, is now the Antlers Inn. It is located at the crest of the road in Twin Peaks. (R.)

On the highest spot of Twin Peaks sits the Strawberry Peak Fire Lookout. It has spotted many of the fires that have threatened Crestline and the other mountaintop resort towns. Some of the larger fires include the Bear Fire in 1956, the Panorama Fire in 1980, and the Old Fire in 2003. Early detection of a fire brings swift response and has saved lives. (R.)

95

Agua Fria was established in 1917 by the Los Angeles Pacific Electric Train Line as a vacation camp for their employees. The electric trains, often called the Red Cars, operated throughout the Los Angeles area and had tracks that ran all the way to San Bernardino. Buses would bring the employees up the mountain for their vacations. (R.)

Many of the Pacific Electric employees enjoyed the area so much they purchased property and built cabins next to the campgrounds so they could use the lodge and other camp facilities. When it closed, the employees would come to visit their own cabins. Property in the 1930s and 1940s was $10 down and $10 per month in Agua Fria. The town's name means "cold water" in Spanish.(R.)

Blue Jay is located on the west shore of Lake Arrowhead and began as a sawmill before becoming a campground known as Wixom's Corner. Art and Nora Wixom named their camp "Blue Jay" after the Stellar's Jay birds found in the area. In 1934, the 22-acre camp was sold to Stoney DeMent, who expanded the store and restaurant. This is Blue Jay in the 1940s.

Blue Jay is well known for ice skating. Harry Leuthold first created a shallow pond for winter skating in the 1920s. In 1938, Stoney DeMent built an ice rink in Blue Jay (shown here). The Ice Castle public rink opened in the early 1980s but closed when the roof collapsed in the winter of 2001. The nearby Ice Castle International Training Center has trained Olympic ice skaters, including Michelle Kwan, Sasha Cohen, and Nichole Bobek. The Ice Castle Training Center is currently owned by six-time Australian National Champion Anthony Liu.

Lake Arrowhead was originally called Little Bear Valley when the sawmills of Talmadge, Tyler, Hook, and others were constructed to cut trees in the 1860s. After the Daley Canyon Mountain Turnpike Road was constructed in 1870, Little Bear Valley and surrounding areas had a direct road to the valley. The 1870s to the 1890s were very active years for the sawmills in the region. The Daley Road crossed Highway 18 just west of the high school. (R.)

Lake Arrowhead was the only lake of a proposed seven-lake project to be completed after the builders lost a 1913 lawsuit over diverting water to the valley side of the mountain rather than the desert, as required by law. One of the proposed lake sites was Lake Gregory, shown here. (T.)

Little Bear Fishing Resort, as Lake Arrowhead was called before 1924, became a popular fishing lake with hotels, boats, and campgrounds. The Little Bear Lake Post Office opened in 1917. The reservoir and surrounding area was sold in 1921 to the Arrowhead Lake Company. (R.)

The Arrowhead Lake Company tore down all the old buildings and created a new, modern, upscale resort with a French-Norman-style village with parking for automobiles. Over $8 million was spent building Lake Arrowhead Village. It opened on June 24, 1922, with a dance pavilion, shopping, restaurants, and an outdoor movie theater. Electricity was generated by the dam and wired to all the buildings and the water supply was drawn from "deep inside the clear, cool lake." (R.)

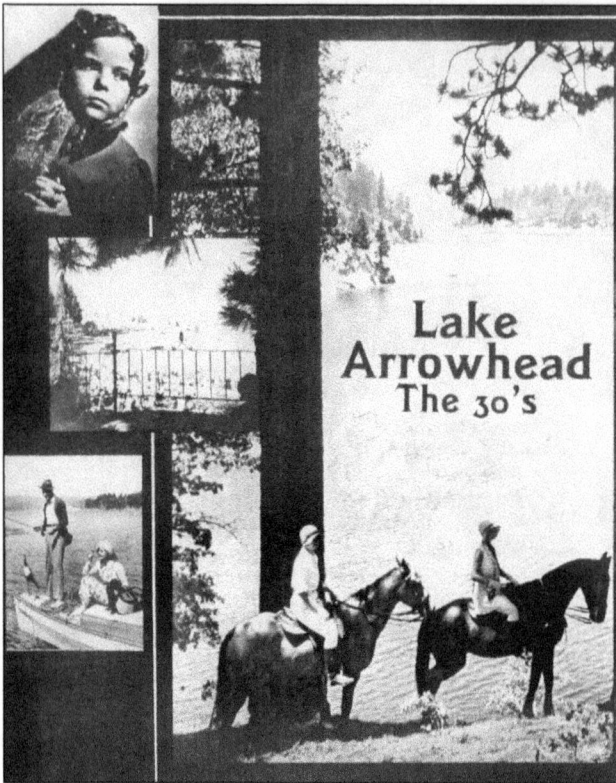

Lake Arrowhead has created an image as an upscale resort. Over 50 movies have been filmed on the lake and surrounding forest. The privately owned lake offers waterskiing, wakeboarding, sailing, motorboating, and fishing activities for its property owners. (R.)

Lake Arrowhead Village was sold in 1978, and the new owners allowed the local fire department to burn down most of the old village in a series of firefighting exercises. A new village was constructed on the lakefront site in the early 1980s, retaining only the original round dance pavilion/arcade (shown). Lake Arrowhead now attracts hundreds of thousands of visitors yearly. (CC.)

Seven

BUILDING THE COMMUNITY

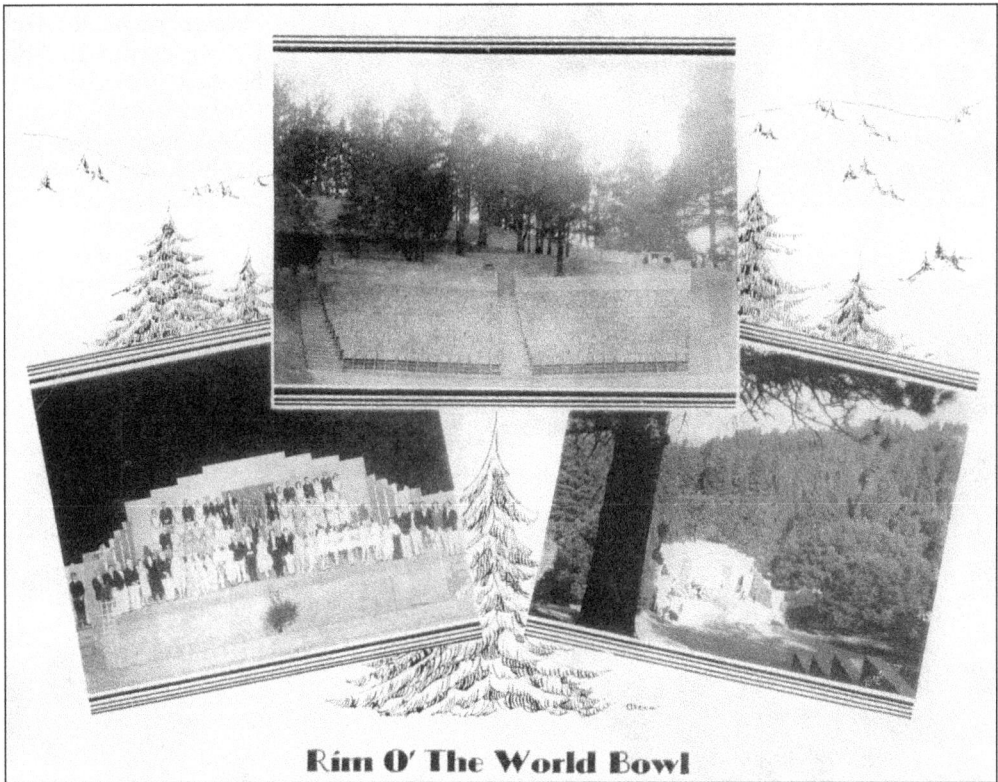

Rim O' The World Bowl

As the 1920s began, there were only about 19 families who resided from Cedarpines Park to Strawberry Peak. John Adams had strung a phone line between the homes. After World War II, the subdivision era began and Crestline received a post office. The town of Crestline, officially named in 1919, began to grow around the stage stop and Samuel Dillin's store. The Skyland and Crestline developments began to flourish, as did many businesses. The first year-round families created the direction and momentum of the community. The Rim of the World Club was the first community association to promote the group vision for the growing community. The Rim of the World Bowl was an amphitheater built by developer Charles S. Mann to promote the Crestline area and to provide entertainment for locals and visitors alike. The Depression led to the demise of this public facility.(T.)

101

One of the early 20th-century visitors and homeowners in the Skyland area was western movie star Leo Maloney (center), a contemporary of Tom Mix. He liked the area so much he purchased several acres and built a silent western movie set and studio in an area he called Skyland Flats, located in the valley below Skyland (now identified as near Huston Flat where Lake Drive goes through the business district of Lake Gregory Village). This is Maloney in action in the 1926 silent movie *Without Orders*. (T.)

It's said that Leo Maloney spent over $100,000 building his Western movie set and production facilities. Maloney filmed over 12 movies there from 1926 through 1928 and rented out the sets to other film companies as well. Some of the other movies shot there include the *High Hand* and *Outlaw Express*, both in 1926, and *Long Loop of the Pecos* in 1927. The set was approximately where the corner of Lake Drive and Alder are today. Local residents, such as Don Handley, were often used as extras. (S; R.)

Over the years many other movie stars have owned homes in the Crestline area, including Bela Lugosi and Lucille Ball, both who had homes in Skyland. Clara Bow, the "it girl," owned a vacation cabin the in the Valley of Enchantment. Hollywood's Delmar Davies built this hunting lodge in the Playground area along the Rim. Since Shirley Temple, who made four movies in the area, was his frequent guest, it is called the Shirley Temple House. (Rose Wiegand.)

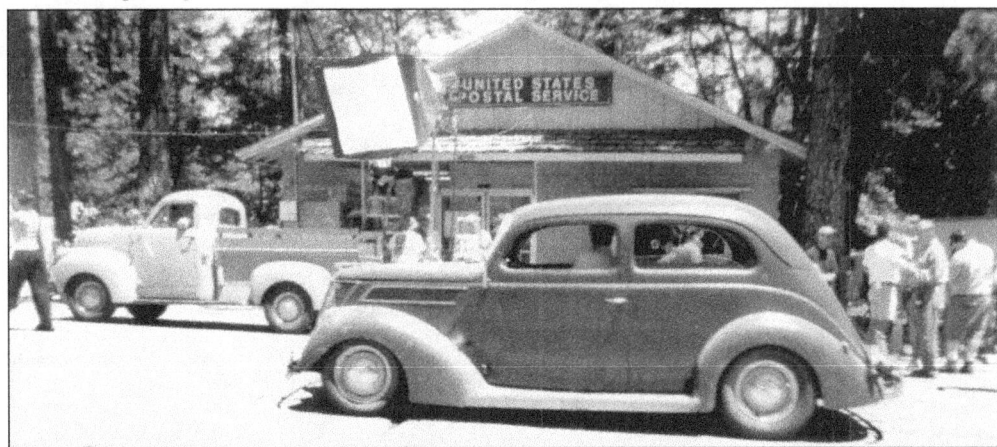

Several movies have been filmed in part in the Crestline area during the last 25 years, including the *Hand*, directed by Oliver Stone, in 1980. *Walk Like a Man*, starring Howie Mandel, was filmed in Crestline in 1986. In 1997, Disney's remake of the *Parent Trap* was filmed in Crestline. Disney hired almost 100 local schoolgirls as extras and had a premiere for them at the Crestline Village Movie Theater. In this 2002 photograph, the television show *Star Trek: Enterprise* is shooting an episode in the Valley of Enchantment. (T.)

The first school in the Crest Forest area was in operation during the 1860 summer cutting season of the James Sawmill. J. J. Willis was the teacher who taught children of the sawmill workers in a cabin built to house the school. This monument on Lake Drive honors education as being very important, even during the early days in the mountains. It was installed by the Crest Forest Historical Society with help from So Cal Edison. The workers shown, from left to right, are (front row) Vince Jacobo, Dan Staple, Dennis Cole, and Lou McGahan; and (standing) Kent Dunn, Richard Guill, Tom Powell Jr., and Charlie Clifford. This log round has since been replaced with a smaller one. (R.)

The Crest School District formed in 1913 and joined the Summit School District in 1918. The other school in the district was located in Summit Valley. The school building in Cedar Pines Park was in operation during the 1920s until 1929, when the new school board had two members from the Crestline area elected. They closed both Summit District schools and opened a new school in Crestline to serve the seven students in the area. The former Cedar Pines Park School is now used as the Cedarpines Park Community Center. (T.)

The first Crest Forest School was located in a house on the hill behind the post office. The Crest Forest District purchased some lots and Charles S. Mann and the forest service donated other lots to create the campus on Crestline Road. The next year a two-room wooden building was constructed. The cafeteria and gymnasium were built next, and then the modern cement four-room school came, which was completed by 1942. (T.)

The Crest Forest School has grown with a two-story addition and portable classrooms. The school originally served grades one through eight and then only housed grades four through eight when the Valley Of Enchantment School was built. The name of the Crest Forest School was changed to Mary Tone School in 1974 to honor everyone's favorite kindergarten teacher. Miss Tone came to Crestline during World War II as an aircraft mechanic at San Bernardino's Norton Air Force Base. After the war, she began teaching and became beloved in the community. The campus currently houses Mountain High School, Alpine Adult Education, and the Rim of the World home schooling programs. (T.)

The Crest Forest School District unified with the Lake Arrowhead and Running Springs School Districts to form the Rim of the World School District in 1957. Rim of the World High School was built and had its first graduating class of 40 students in 1957. This enabled children the chance to attend high school on the mountain instead of boarding in San Bernardino while attending San Bernardino High School during the weekdays. Pictured here is a Crestline school bus. (R.)

The Valley of Enchantment Elementary School, constructed in the 1960s, was designed for grades kindergarten through three. This picture shows the school when it only had four classrooms. Mary Tone taught kindergarten for many years in the downstairs classroom at the Crest Forest School and then finished her career teaching at the Valley of Enchantment Elementary School. (T.)

The newest school in Crestline was constructed in 1996 near the eastern shore of Lake Gregory. It replaced Mary Tone Elementary because more classrooms were needed as the population of the community grew. The old, two-story school could not be made handicapped-accessible with its multiple level playgrounds, as it was built on a hillside. Lake Gregory Elementary School has an elevator and provides education for grades four through six. (T.)

Crestline has several wall murals to enhance the beauty of the community and to share some of the heritage of the town. In this triptych, the above mural (located at Lake Drive) shows a peaceful lake and forest scene. The second mural, at the corner of Lake and Lake Gregory Drives across the lake, has three scenes. One shows students waiting for a school bus at the Alpine Glens Resort, the first Crest Forest Fire Station, and the Old Rim of the World Road. Inside the Crestline Library, pictured below, is a large brown-tone painting. The canvas was painted in 1919 and was one in a four-painting diorama used to decorate the walls of the dining room at the Hotel Tetley in Riverside. The paintings were used to promote the sales of mountain vacation property from the 1920s to the 1950s. (T.)

For many years, the Native Sons of the Golden West had a meeting hall located at the corner of Seely Flat Road and Huston Flat Road (Highway 138 and Lake Drive), just north of Crest Forest Drive. They placed numerous historical monuments around town, of which three are now located at the building's entrance. Pictured above is one of the Switzerland Monuments (top portion of the photo) that were built to designate the gates to the Club San Moritz properties on Lake Drive, the Mormon Springs Water Well Monument erected 1933 (bottom left), the Doyle Memorial and Hydraulic Mining monument plaques dated 1928 and 1933 (middle), and the Charles S. Mann Memorial of 1940 (T.)

Over 250 films have been shot in the San Bernardino Mountains since the days of silent movies. The museum's "star wall" has photographs of some of the actors who made movies in the local area. Pictured, clockwise from the top, are Wallace Reid, William S. Hart, Shirley Temple, Broncho Billy Anderson, Gary Cooper, Lon Chaney, and Mary Pickford. The museum was inspired by the book *Those Magnificent Mountain Movies* by Lee Cozad. (T.)

The original movie projector used in the Crestline Village Theater, where the museum is located, is on display there. It is a Simplex Super Motion Picture Projector that uses a carbon arc lamp. The carbon rods would burn to create the brightness required to project the image the length of the theater, which was constructed in a World War II–era quanset hut.

Crest Forest Fire District was formed in 1929. The Rim of the World Club, along with 72 property owners, petitioned the San Bernardino County Board of Supervisors to set up a fire-protection district. It was to cover Blue Jay to Cedar Pines Park, an area of 19.5 square miles that is surrounded by a national forest. The first meeting of the Crest Forest Fire District was held at John Baylis's Pinecrest Resort, where he was elected president of the commission. John Nardi from Cedarpines Park, Fred Spencer of Thousand Pines, B. W. Switzer of Twin Peaks, and Frank Russell of Crestline were the fire commissioners. There was one full-time inspector and 18 volunteer firefighters. The budget for the first year, which included the purchase of three engines, was $8,076. (T; G.)

The first fire engines purchased had Studebaker chassis with standard water pumps, which had a capacity of pumping 105 gallons per minute with 120 pounds of water pressure. The trucks got three miles per gallon of gasoline, but the first year only $360 was spent on gas, oil, and repairs. Here is Joe Bertucci in the driver's seat and Frank Nardi on the running board at Fire Station Number 1 in Cedar Pines Park. (R.)

110

Fire Station Number 2 was built on the main street between the tavern and post office and Russell's Hardware store in Crestline. Fire Company Number 3 was located in Twin Peaks, across from the Alpine Glens Resort (now known as the Antlers). The stations were strategically located for quick volunteer response to anywhere in the fire district. Here are all three engines (and another vehicle) in front of the Crestline station with the fire-fighting volunteers and their families. (R.)

Titled "Monday Morning Fire Drill," this shows Crest Forest Drive in 1944 looking west, with the fire hoses laid out to dry in front of Station Number 2. (G.)

Firefighters show off the new fire trucks and the strong water pressure of the new equipment to firefighters and family members at Moon Lake in 1929. For several years an engine was stationed in the Valley of the Moon for the volunteers to use. (R.)

Standing in front of the second Crest Forest Fire Station Number 2 in 1948 are members of the volunteer fire crew including (left to right) Lee Morre, unidentified, Bob, Lalo Cadona. unidentified, Pete Best, Mr Chalker, Elmer Springer, unidentified, and Wes Hooley. This building was replaced by the new Crest Forest Fire District Headquarters and Fire Station, which opened in July 2000. (G.)

By the 1960s, there were 12 volunteer companies, with 125 paid call firefighters. These volunteers felt a responsibility to protect the community they lived and worked in and they dedicated many hours to training. In the center is 1964 Fire Chief Francis Newcomb and the fire commissioners. Frank Nardi, who was still with the fire district, is sitting in the old 1929 fire truck from Cedarpines Park Station Number 1. (G; T.)

The first full-time Crest Forest fire chief was hired in 1950, not long after the Rim of the World Inn/Lodge, located near the corner of Crest Forest Drive and Highway 138, burned to the ground. The gas station shown was built on the location of the former park. Murphy's Dance Hall can be seen beyond it. Many years later, Linder Tire was built on that site. (G; T.)

This 1987 photograph showcases all the equipment and personnel of the full-time and paid-call firefighters of the Crest Forest Fire District sitting in the south parking lot of Lake Gregory. (G; T.)

The Crest Forest Fire District has saved the town of Crestline from the ravages of fire many times, including the Panorama Fire in 1980 and the Old Fire in 2003. Though some structures were lost in 2003, if it had not been for the skills of the Crest Forest Fire District personnel and their knowledge of local wind patterns, landscapes, and terrain, the whole town could have been lost to the fire. Residents of Skyland, which lost 33 homes in the 2003 Old Fire, were still rebuilding in 2005. (LR.)

The Fourth of July has been celebrated in grand style since the days of the sawmills, when families of the workers would come up to the mountains for several days of camping, barbequing, and friendly competition that featured relay races between the mill workers. Crestline has continued the tradition of holding festivals and competitions over the Fourth of July weekend. Sawmill Days, Alpine Days, and Jamboree Days all have invited visitors up the mountain to enjoy the weather, vendor's booths, events, and parades.

For many years, an honorary mayor was elected during Jamboree Days. Tom Powell Jr. was given the nod in 1986 and pledged to form a historical society. He won the election and he fulfilled his promise. The Jamboree Days Parade is a small-town parade with often over 100 entrants. Many children who grow up in Crestline get the opportunity to be in the parade at least once and have fun throwing candy out to their friends lining the route. (T.)

Eight

FUN IN THE MOUNTAINS

Over the years, most people came to Crestline for a vacation to relax from the humdrum world of lower elevations. The cool breezes through the trees in the forest, the open land, and a feeling of being close to nature appealed to city dwellers of Southern California and their desire to get connected with the environment. Scenically, Crestline offers views of Mount San Jaciento, Mount San Gorgonio, Mount Baldy, and Saddleback Peak. On clear days, downtown Los Angeles, Catalina Island in the Pacific Ocean, and the Mojave Desert can all be seen from various parts of the community. At night the city lights of the San Bernardino Valley and the desert communities can be seen twinkling below.

The Heart Rock Trail is about one mile long, running alongside Seeley Creek, and ends at a lovely waterfall that cascades into a small pond near the Valley of Enchantment. The waterfall has a depression caused by years of heavy rains that looks like a heart, hence the name Heart Rock. The trail and creek, which are located close to Camp Seeley, were used for the filming of the 1997 Disney movie remake of the *Parent Trap*. (T.)

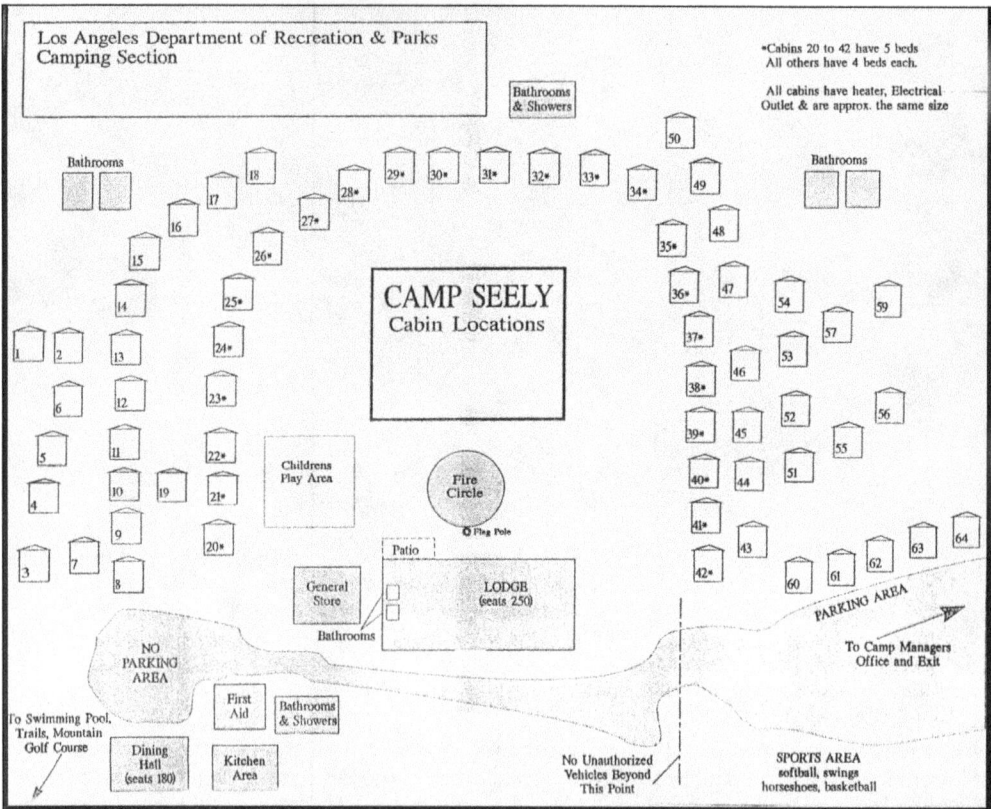

Los Angeles Department of Recreation & Parks
Camping Section

*Cabins 20 to 42 have 5 beds
All others have 4 beds each.

All cabins have heater, Electrical Outlet & are approx. the same size

CAMP SEELY
Cabin Locations

The map of Camp Seeley shows the location of all the cabins in the horseshoe. Over 1 million campers have visited and stayed at Camp Seeley since it opened in 1914. During the Depression, many homeless families made their summer homes at the camp, which is run by the City of Los Angeles. John and Ida Adams, who lived across the street from the camp, cooked meals during those hard-luck years. (T.)

Horseback riders are leaving for a trail ride from Camp Seeley in the 1950s. An equestrian trail around Lake Gregory was built during the 1940s and operated through the 1960s. Now there is a walking trail with fitness exercise stations around Lake Gregory. The fitness trail was constructed in the 1980s by local service clubs and is maintained by the regional park. (T.)

There were also many forest trails leading out from Dart Canyon, Cedar Pines Park, and the Valley of Enchantment. The VOE Stables (shown here) are where many locally owned horses were housed. Horseback riding was popular for many generations in Crestline. (T.)

Vacationland

Miniature Golf And Arcade

ke Drive   Crest

This ad for Vacationland Miniature Golf Course reflects the popularity of the sport during the 1950s through the 1970s. The pinball arcade building has since been converted into a garden center. The arcade was very popular with teens on vacation with their families. (T.)

The Frontier Miniature Golf Course was in the Valley of Enchantment, across the street from Johnnies Market. The arcade building is now a U.S. Postal Service substation. Club San Moritz had a Pitch and Putt Golf Course that was open to the public, with a driving range and miniature golf course as well. The Valley of Enchantment Mobile Home Park was built in that location when the club closed down in the 1970s. (T.)

120

Fishing was a popular draw to the mountain area from the earliest days. Before Lake Gregory was built in 1938, stream fishing was the lure. Huston Creek had a "pay-to-fish" business before Lake Gregory was completed. (R.)

Lake Gregory was immediately popular for fishing, beginning in its first summer. The lake is stocked yearly with catfish and trout. The regional park rents boats for fishing and many a childhood memory had been created while fishing with dad at Lake Gregory. This dock is at the Club San Moritz end of the lake, showing the canals in the background where the San Moritz ball field is now located. (R.)

The beach at Lake Gregory was created when local residents brought up truckloads of sand from the Santa Ana River wash near Redlands. Many a sunburn has been received and tan shown off at Lake Gregory since 1938. (T.)

The side-wheel-paddle tour boat and the many rental items such as paddle boards, pedal boats, sail boats, and other floating devices helped create many happy childhood memories on Lake Gregory over the years. The waterslide, shuffleboard courts, and other activities have made Lake Gregory Regional Park a summertime favorite since it opened in June 1977. (T.)

The Lake Gregory Excursion Boat toured the lake hourly and would take Club San Moritz members over to their beach and drop them off. (R.)

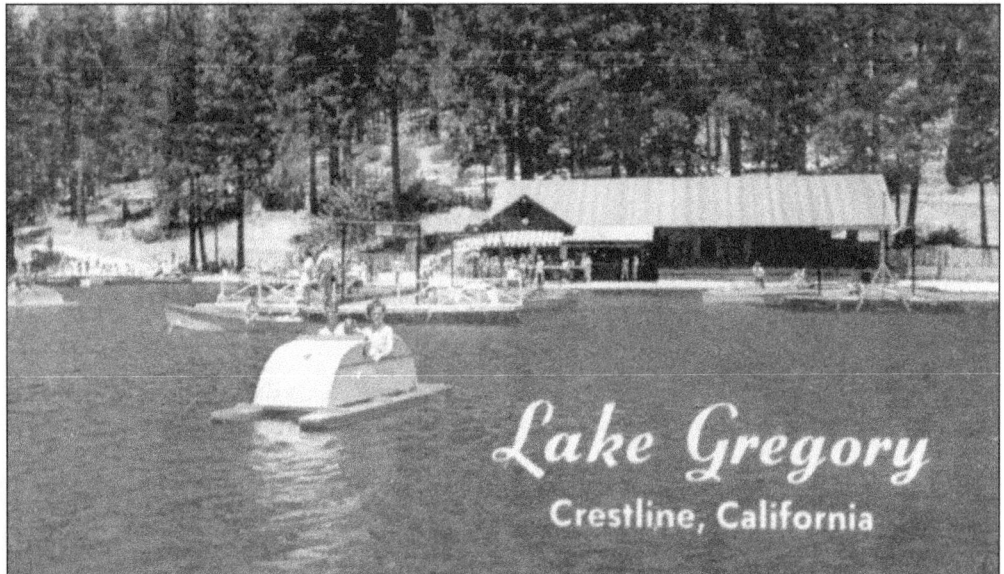

The pedal boats were chain-driven and operated by human cycling power, similar to riding a bicycle. They were rented and could be taken anywhere on the lake from the 1940s to the 1970s. (T.)

After Lake Gregory became a San Bernardino County Regional Park in the late 1970s, new activities including shuffleboard and horseshoes were added. The largest change made by the regional park was the addition of a giant, two-flume water slide. The fountains on the south shore help aerate the water for the fish. Healthy fish are more fun to catch. (R.)

The big plastic slide was located next to the movie theater on Lake Drive during the summer seasons of the 1960s. Climbing the stairs to the top, holding a gunnysack to slide down on, was a childhood memory of both excitement and fear when looking down from the top. This was years before the waterslide was built on Lake Gregory. (T.)

Crestline's original bowling alley was also the legion hall and Sportland Cafe. It was located in Old Town Crestline at the northeast corner of the intersection of Highway 138, Crest Forest Drive, and Lake Drive. It now houses a pizza restaurant and bar. Next door is a building that no longer exists, and further down is Weber's Grocery (now known as Hilltop Liquor).

The Crestline Bowling Alley was also known as Gregory Lanes and Rim Lanes. It has offered league games and fun for local and visiting kids since it was built on Lake Drive in the 1970s. (T.)

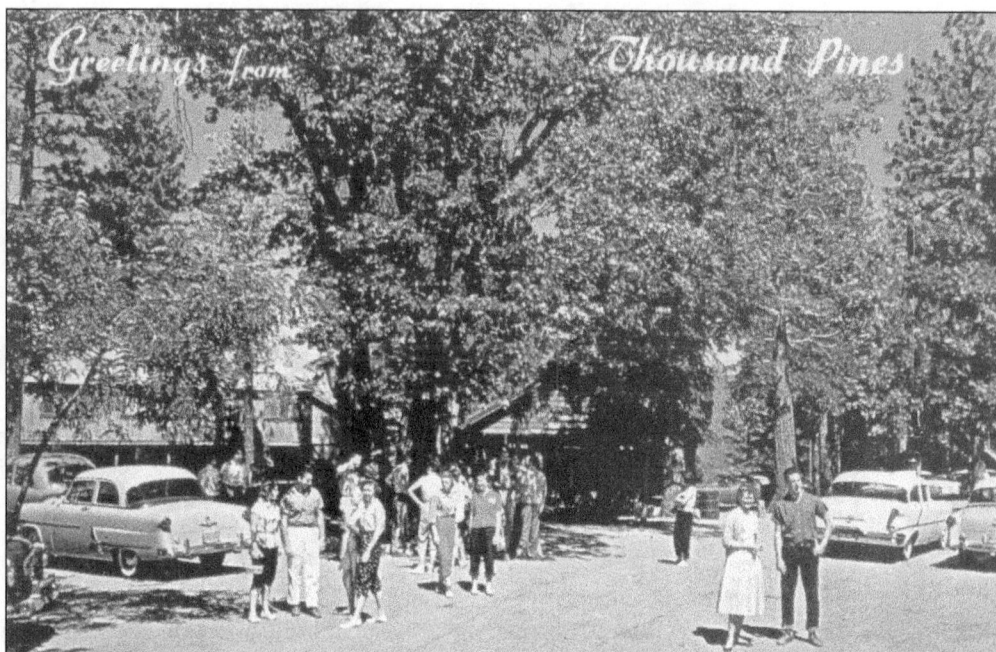

There have been and still are many group campgrounds adjacent to the national forest in the Crestline area. Originally the site of a sawmill, Thousand Pines Camp was established in the 1890s as a family campground. It was owned by Arthur Gregory during the 1930s and was the site where WPA workers lived while building Lake Gregory Dam. It was the site of 1932's 49er Days Celebration. Gregory donated the 150-acre camp to the Baptist Church shortly before his death and it remains today as a popular church camp, which helps to support the local community. It is but one of the many private group camps in Crestline. (T.)

Ohrman's Resort and Campground in the Valley of Enchantment, also known as Crestline Mountain Park, was an 18-acre campground for tent campers, trailer owners, and RV enthusiasts through the 1990s. It had a swimming pool and a recreation and teen center. Many families returned to the campground year after year for family vacations. The acreage is now owned by the Rim of the World School District and may become the site of a new elementary school. (T.)

Camp Paivika, operated by the Crippled Children's Association, is a place where handicapped children have the opportunity to enjoy a true camping experience, even if it's under a doctor's care. The entire camp is handicapped accessible. The zoo room, as it looked in 1964, was so named because of its appearance like a zoo cage. It overlooks the vast valley below. (T.)

Crestline also has had its share of motels with little cabanas for the visitors to relax in. Names from the 1950s and 1960s, such as Woody's Motel, Custer's Lodge, Adams' Caverns, Tangled Pines Cabins, the Whitely Motel, Moon Lodge, and the Sleepy Hollow Cabins evoke summer and wintertime vacation memories in thousands of Southern Californians. (T.)

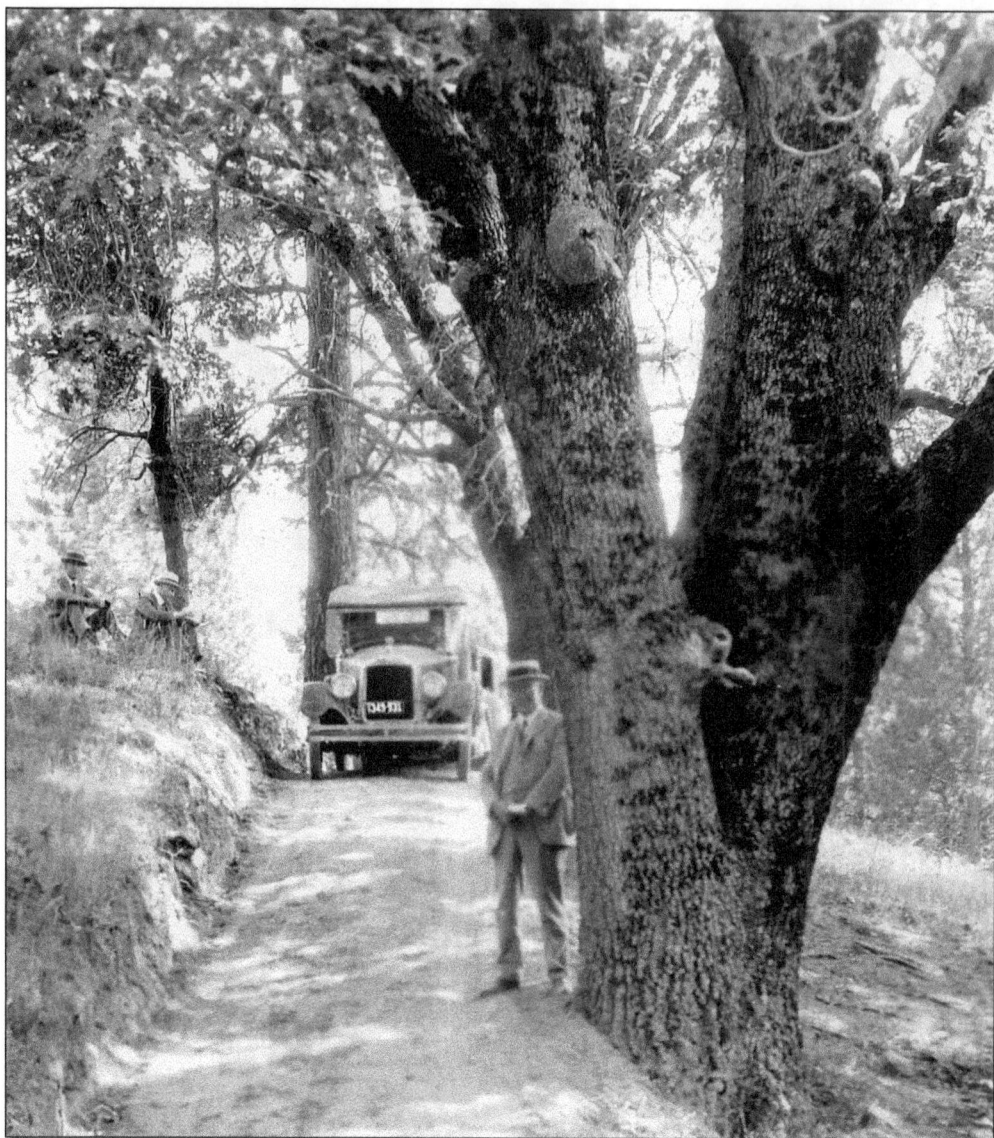

Is it the altitude or attitude that makes Crestline a unique place? Many say it is a mixture of both, along with a splash of the personalities of people who have developed, lived in, and loved the town. State Road Commissioner Frank Tetley Sr. (shown here leaning against a tree), who developed the Rim of the World Park (later known as the Valley of Enchantment) as a vacation getaway destination in the 1920s, would be surprised to see the full-time, year-round community Crestline has become. (T.)

www.ingramcontent.com/pod-product-compliance
Lightning Source LLC
Chambersburg PA
CBHW080616110426
42813CB00006B/1526